The God
You Need to Know

Discover His Story, Experience His Love

Linda Evans Shepherd

The God You Need to Know

Copyright © 2017 Linda Evans Shepherd

Some names and details have been changed to protect privacy.

In most scenes using Biblical dialogue, the dialogue is taken directly from Scripture. On occasion, the dialogue is modified for purposes of editing and clarity.

Published by EA Books Publishing a division of
Living Parables of Central Florida, Inc. a 501c3
EABooksPublishing.com

DEDICATION

To my sweet daughter, Laura.
You spend your days walking with God.

CONTENTS

ACKNOWLEDGMENTS

I acknowledge this manuscript (my very favorite to date) has faced more setbacks to publication than any of my thirty published books. And now, after six years of delays, I thank the good Lord for seeing *The God You Need To Know* through to completion as I believe it contains powerful truths that will transform lives.

Secondly, I thank Cheri Cowell and EA Books Publishing, Inc., as well as Angela Breidenback for all their help.

With Love,
Linda Evans Shepherd
www.EnjoyGodStory.com

INTRODUCTION

Divine Focus

"People whose eyes are riveted on themselves cannot focus upon God." George Barna[1]

Are you ready to enter into the mystery of experiencing God's love story for you? Then it's time to learn how to focus on him in every area of your life. This kind of focus will connect you with God, help you overcome the darkness, and help you experience God's love, peace, and victory. For the battle raging around us is not won in hand-to-hand combat, but through the lifting of our eyes to God (Ps. 124:8).

Coming Attractions

Before I share the secrets of how to get into step with God, I want to tell you the most magnificent story ever told so you can experience the beauty, majesty, and wonder of God and all that is holy, divine, and sacred. As you watch *The God You Need To Know*, my hope is you will fall headfirst into God's love. But to accomplish this mission and to experience all the secrets this book has to share, pray this:

Dear Lord,

I invite you to join me as I read this book. Please anoint me to learn your truth. Help me to take my eyes off my own circumstances and to focus entirely on you.

And now to you, who is above and beyond what words can describe or minds can comprehend; I offer you my love and attention. I offer you my respect and reverence. You are majestic and holy. You are worthy of my love.

---

[1] George Barna quote, *Inside Out Worship; Insights for Passionate and Purposeful Worship* by Matt Redman (Ventura, CA: Heart of Worship Trust, Regal Books from Gospel Light, 2005), P.123.

Teach me to love you more deeply and to worship you in both spirit and truth. Teach me how to understand and live your love story for me.

In Jesus' Name

Amen

Chapter 1

Divine Beginnings

"Let us run with endurance the race God has set before us."
Hebrews 12:1b NLT

Have you ever wanted to better understand God's story?

You can. In the next few pages you'll get the chance to view the story of God as if we are watching a movie together.

The Opening Act

The story you're about to see may be familiar. It's about how a loving God created, lost, and then reclaimed a deep friendship with those he created. It's a story as old as the universe but so fresh it still plays in hearts everywhere. I'm pleased to bring this galactic production to the theater of your mind. But first, let me plop into the recliner next to yours and press the power button on the remote, *this is going to be good...*

...*"The God You Need To Know"* scrolls across our big screen in large, gold letters. Look at the disclaimer, "This production is only a facsimile of the glory of heaven and the splendor of God which is more awesome than can possibly be portrayed here."

Listen to the sounds of the heavenly choir swell through our surround sound. We're squinting as light pulsates from our big screen. As the camera comes into focus, we can make out the faces of the singers. *Angels!*

They don't look much like the angels on our Christmas cards, do they? They're tall, almost warlike with gleaming

1

wings. But despite their formidable appearance, their voices have tones of purity and beauty that melt our hearts.

Do you see to whom they're singing? It's Jehovah, the Lord God Almighty.

He's on his throne, surrounded by what appears to be a rainbow of living colors over a sea of crystal. This is so glorious and part of the glory is the worship music itself; it's alive and saturates our very being.

Look at the choir director. He's the most magnificent angel of all. He's so radiant that he's known as the Dawn of Heaven. But he's got something on his face. Could it be? Yes, the Dawn of Heaven, a.k.a Satan, wears a sneer of pride as he plans to hijack the angelic worship for himself.

I'll press the fast-forward button so we can watch the images whirl by. Look; Satan is leading one-third of the heavenly angels into war against Jehovah. When he loses the battle he's tossed out of heaven along with his angelic followers. See how they tumble through time and space as they plummet to planet earth (Ezekiel 28:12-17)?

Now the scene is morphing. The fallen angels have descended into a void of darkness. The picture fades to black until God says, "Let there be light."

Ah! We've arrived at the birth of creation. Notice God's spirit hovering over the earth as he separates the light from the darkness, the muck from the mire, and the sky from the water. Watch this incredible footage of God as he creates green plants and delicate blossoms. Observe as He designs a variety of living creatures beneath a periwinkle blue sky that slowly fades into a star-filled night.

Listen! In the new dawn you can hear creation hum its praises to God as He fashions man out of earth and woman from man's rib. Look at this newly formed couple God so tenderly loves. How beautiful and joyful they are! God walks and talks with them in the cool of the evening.

But wait. There, slinking out of the shadows by the spring—isn't that Satan disguised as a dazzling bird? Are you surprised he doesn't look like a snake? (Remember he wasn't cursed to crawl on the ground until the end of this scene.) But what is he doing talking to the woman, Eve?

Let's listen in…

…The two sit together relaxing on a warm rock in the late afternoon sun. They watch water bubble into a clear pool filled with bright fish. As the spring babbles, blue butterflies dance in the nearby blossoms. The serpent, the most beautiful creature in the garden, ruffles his iridescent feathers of green and turquoise and leans into Eve's ear. He gently whispers, "Did God really say, 'You must not eat from any tree in the garden?'"

A look of astonishment reflects in Eve's large, brown eyes and she glides her hand cross the surface of the water as she contemplates her answer. How had this creature known to ask her the very question she'd so often wondered?

Feeling as though she's found a confidante, she lowers her voice. "We may eat fruit from the trees in the garden, but God did say, 'You must not eat fruit from the tree that is in the middle of the garden.'" She pauses before adding her own twist, "and you must not touch it, or you will *die.*"

The serpent clucks its tongue and gazes into Eve's trusting eyes. "You will not surely die. For God knows that when you eat of it your eyes will be opened, and you will be like God, knowing good and evil" (Gen 3:1-5).

Freeze fame. This, my friend, is the original lie, a lie powered with Satan's favorite motivator—pride.

But will Eve swallow it?…

…She bites into the forbidden fruit and its sticky juice runs down her bare arm. She does not yet realize she's been poisoned so she offers Adam a bite. He too sinks his teeth into the toxic fruit.

As sin starts to course through their veins, their eyes are opened. They *can* see; they see they have sinned against God in this act of willful disobedience.

I'll fast forward to the cool of the evening when God arrives to walk with this young couple.

"Adam? Eve? Where are you?"

In the silence we can see they are hiding deep in the foliage, ashamed of their nakedness, ashamed to stand exposed before the holiness of God.

When God finds them cowering in the shrubbery, he's both angry and heartbroken. Their disobedience has created a galactic dilemma. You see, God is so holy he cannot walk with sin. He has no choice but to banish Adam and Eve from his presence.

It's a gut-wrenching scene. Heartbroken, God turns his back as Adam and Eve stumble away from their best friend to face a world without his dear presence.

The camera refocuses on Satan, that old deceiver. Despite the fact God cursed his disguise to forever slither on its belly, he's won a great victory. Though he may have previously lost the glory of heaven, he now has power over God's beloved children. He has won the right to steal, kill and to destroy.

Act Two

I'm fast-forwarding through time again.

Shield your eyes or you'll see the tragic scene where Adam and Eve's son, Cain, kills his brother, Abel. How horrible! Even as Abel's blood pools on the ground, this murder foreshadows the wickedness that will dominate the earth. Man's evil continues to grow until God washes the world clean with a great flood (Gen 7.) Let's watch as Noah and his sons answer God's call to build an ark. See how God sends the animals to board Noah's hand-hewed boat? In this next scene, the rain pours from the skies, colliding with boiling waters that rush from the deep in a great flood that sweeps the earth. Noah's floating zoo bobs through the waves as God's wrath splashes over the tallest mountain peaks and drowns a wicked generation.

Unfortunately God's do-over does little to resolve the problem of sin. Sin still lives in the hearts of Noah and his family, as well as their descendents.

Finally generations later, God unveils a foreshadowing of his master plan to rescue us. As I queue this scene for you, be warned it contains a river of blood. Here we see God's priests as they continually sacrifice bulls, lambs, and goats on the altar of God's temple in an attempt to use the blood of animals to cover the sins of God's people. However, this blood serves as a temporary solution. The problem is this blood is not holy and cannot continually cover the sins God's people commit. As this scene ends, God's people are still naked and ashamed.

You might ask; then is there no hope, no hero to save us? Will we be separated from God forever? Behold...

Act Three

...An angel appears in the night sky and hovers over a band of frightened shepherds. "Do not be afraid. I bring you good news of great joy that will be for all people. Today in the town of David a Savior has been born to you; he is Christ the Lord. This will be a sign to you: You will find a baby wrapped in cloths and lying in a manger."

The sky brightens as angels sing, "Glory to God in the highest, and on earth peace to men on whom his favor rests" (Luke 2:10-14).

But not everyone enjoys the music. Look, Satan watches with distain. He must be thinking, *How dare the choir I once directed worship a human baby, instead of me!*

The camera pans to a stable in Bethlehem where a newborn baby sleeps in a manger. How precious he is! But this Jesus is no ordinary child. This is the second Adam. This one, who peacefully sleeps, came from heaven to carry out a mission; a rescue mission so humankind can once again walk with God.

This mission was made possible because Jesus was born of a virgin. This means he was born outside the curse of sin transmitted through the seed of man. He was sired, not by man, but by God's Holy Spirit to become God's only begotten son.

These next few scenes are delightful – Jesus grows from a baby to a young man. He's the perfect child; perfect because he is not under the curse of sin like the rest of us. Sinless, he grows in the knowledge and wisdom of God.

Let's slow down as Jesus, now thirty, is tested by Satan. Satan takes Jesus to a very high mountain and shows him the splendor of all the kingdoms of the world. "All this I will give you, if you will bow down and worship me."

Jesus gazes across the grandeur before him but refuses to fall for Satan's snare of pride. "Away from me, Satan! For it is written: 'Worship the Lord your God, and serve him only.'"

Jesus passed this crucial test and now the game is on. At stake? All of mankind.

Why does God consider man such a prize? Because God longs for us. He misses the walks he once shared with us in the cool of the evening. He wants to win us from the dominion of Satan, because unlike Satan, He really loves us.

On the other hand, Satan wants control of us out of revenge for God. He wants to destroy us and break God's heart. He's determined our lives will be lived as a sacrifice to him.

The Divine Mission

Let's watch as Jesus teaches the secrets of the kingdom of heaven to the men and women who sit at his feet on the hillside. He says,

> "Blessed are the poor in spirit, for theirs is the kingdom of heaven. Blessed are those who mourn, for they will be comforted. Blessed are the meek, for they will inherit the earth. Blessed are those who hunger and thirst for righteousness, for they will be filled. Blessed are the merciful, for they will be shown mercy. Blessed are the pure in heart, for they will see God. Blessed are the peacemakers, for they will be called sons of God. Blessed are those who are persecuted because of righteousness, for theirs is the kingdom of heaven. Blessed are you when people insult you, persecute you and falsely say all kinds of evil against you because of me. Rejoice and be glad, because great is your reward in heaven, for in the same way they persecuted the prophets who were before you" (Matt 5:3-12).

What a message. But look in the fringes of the crowd where the religious leaders lurk. You'd think Jesus would welcome these "holy" men in an effort to gain their approval. Instead of playing politics, he says what he *really* thinks, "Woe to you, teachers of the law and Pharisees, you hypocrites! You clean the outside of the cup and dish, but inside they are full of greed and self-indulgence. Blind Pharisee! First clean the inside of the cup and dish, and then the outside also will be clean" (Matt 23:25-26).

He insulted them? No wonder these leaders plot to kill him. No wonder they send a Roman guard to arrest him in the Garden of Gethsemane and drag him into court. There's Jesus standing quietly before these same men as they determine if he will live or die. The head priest gives Jesus a sideways glare, "Are you then the Son of God?"

Jesus answers, "You are right in saying *I AM.*"

The priest and his council tear their robes and cry out, "Why do we need any more testimony? We have heard it from his own lips" (Luke 22:70-71).

They are furious because Jesus has just used one of the names for God, "I AM," to describe *himself.* These religious rulers are not only outraged; they have the advantage. They know based on this "violation" of their law they can put Jesus to death. In their minds, Jesus has blasphemed God by equating himself *with* God.

The camera pans away from the trial to the shadows of the earth where we see Satan and his angels in their raucous celebration. Their hate fans the dark hearts of these religious leaders with lust for the death of God's only begotten son. The demons cheer as Jesus is sentenced to death. They join in with the mocks of the crowd as Jesus is beaten, then nailed to the cross.

It's hard not to turn away when we see Jesus hanging on the cross, suspended between life and death.

However Satan is elated. Look how he crows as Jesus takes his last breath. In this moment, the celebration in the shadows of darkness begins. Why the joy? Satan believes the death of Jesus ends all challenge to his power and dominion. He has killed mankind's only hope for salvation; or so he thinks.

Darkness falls. The Roman soldiers guard Jesus' tomb as our camera focuses on the heavy stone that blocks its entrance. The picture fades to black.

Game over.

Or is it?

Three days later an earthquake rattles the land as the one who never sinned steps out of death and into life. The great stone rolls away and glory from the tomb spills into the morning. Before us stands Jesus Christ, the Son of God, the very moment he conquered both sin and death. He is risen. He has set us free from the bonds that held us hostage.

Now, we are no longer naked and ashamed before God. We can choose to be clothed in the purity and innocence of Christ as his robe of righteousness covers our sins. Now we can be counted as sinless and we can once again walk with the Lord of the universe.

We have been set free indeed!

The credits are rolling. Do you see what they say? They list the names of the redeemed, the ones whose lives have been set free from the bonds of Satan. Is your name listed?

If not, *it can be*.

In fact, because Act Three ends with the resurrection of Christ, you can choose the freedom to walk with God or you can choose to stay a slave to the dominion of Satan. In other words, you can choose an eternity with God or you can choose the eternal fires of hell where you will become a forever sacrifice to Satan.

Which will you choose?

Time for Prayer

To answer God's call, to add your name to the credits of the ones saved through the power of the grace of God through the work of Jesus, pray this prayer:

Dear God,

Thank you for sending your son to die for my sins. I put my sins on the sacrificial lamb, Jesus. The blood of Jesus forever washes away my sin so I can walk with you. God, please forgive me. Please give me the power to turn from darkness and to live in your love. Lead me. Teach me how to really know you.

In Jesus' Name

Amen.

If this is the first time you asked God to forgive you of your sins, it's time to celebrate! Shout a thank you, dance, clap, wave at God. Call your grandmother or that lady in the office who told you she's been praying for you. It's time to celebrate and it's time to share your good news.

New Age vs. Divine Truth

Once a New Age friend told me she worshipped creation because "all things are God."

I told her, "I believe something very similar to you. I do not believe all things are God, but rather, I believe God created all things. There's a Scripture in the Bible, 'Through him all things were made; without him nothing was made that has been made'" (John 1:3).

"The Bible also says, 'He is before all things, and in him all things hold together' (Colossians 1:17). I believe God is not only the creator of life, he is the secret force to life itself. He holds all things together."

She seemed intrigued so I continued, "So creation is a lot like me. Creation is not God, but creation displays the power of God in its very being. I too believe I am not God, but I have the power and spirit of God inside of me, because, through Jesus, I've invited God to come into my very being and to forgive me of my sins and now his spirit indwells me. I truly walk with God."

My friend was dumbfounded by this thought. "What you're saying makes sense and it gives me a lot to think about."

And it should. We are not God, we are the created; the very ones who have been chosen to have a friendship with God.

Love Notes:

In this chapter, we can surmise that in order to walk with God we have to understand:

- God's story.

- Why God sent his son to rescue us.

- The Who of whom we worship; he's not the creation, he's the creator.

Now, we are on our way to understanding the living God has called us to walk with him. But first, we worship him. Worship is one of the best possible ways to walk with God.

A Power Walk Experience:

Experience One:

In order to have a greater revelation of God, we'll study some of his 365 names; one for every day of the year. Author Kay Arthur says, "In biblical times, a name represented a person's character. God's name represents His attributes, His nature. His name is a statement of who He is."[2]

In our limited study of God's names, we'll better understand his attributes so we can better worship Him. We'll start with three of his names as we turn our study of his names into a praise experience.

- Jehovah – (juh-HO-vah) – One use of this name is found in Exodus 3:14, "God said to Moses, "I AM WHO I AM. This is what you are to say to the Israelites: 'I AM has sent me to you.'" This name describes God as the one who never changes, never fails, and is faithful to the faithless.[3]

  Praise: Jehovah, you are the great I AM. You are God, worthy of my praise. I praise you Jehovah, and I thank you for being faithful to me when I was faithless. Thank you that you never change; and that you never fail. I give you glory and honor.

- Elohim – (el-o-HEEM) – One use of this name is found in Gen 1:1-2, "In the beginning God (Elohim) created the heavens and the earth. Now the earth was formless and empty, darkness was over the surface of the deep, and the Spirit of God (Elohim) was hovering over the waters." This name describes God as the creator, the all-powerful one. It's plural and thought to describe the personages of God as described by the term "Trinity."[4]

  Praise: Elohim, you are the creator, the all powerful one. You know all, you read every thought, you are

---

[2] Kay Arthur, *The Peace & Power of Knowing God's Name*, (Colorado Springs, CO: Waterbrook Press, 2002), Back cover.
[3] *The Names of God* Wall Chart, (Torrance, CA: RW Research Inc. Rose Publishing Inc., 2003).
[4] Ibid.

present everywhere at all times. My mind cannot comprehend your fullness. To think one so powerful as you wants to walk with someone so tiny as me is—breathtaking. You love me and I praise and I worship you. I bow before you in awe of your glory.

Experience Two:

We will return to our study of the names of God in the chapters that follow. In the next chapter we will talk about walking in love. But in the meantime, we'll take another moment to worship God. Read or sing this old hymn that praises God for his creation:

All Things Bright and Beautiful

All things bright and beautiful,
All creatures great and small,
And all things wise and wonderful;
The Lord God made them all.

Each little flow'r that opens up,
Each little bird that sings,
He made their glowing colors and
He made their tiny wings.

The purple-headed mountain,
The river running by,
The sunset and the morning light
That brightens up the sky.

The cold wind in the wintertime,
The pleasant summer sun,
The ripe fruits in the garden now,
He made them ev'ry one.

He gave us eyes to see them all,
And lips that we might tell
How great is the Almighty God
Who has made all things well.

-- Cecil Frances Alexander (1818-1895)[5]

---

[5] All Things Bright and Beautiful by Cecil Frances Alexander and compiled by Robert K. Brown and Mark R. Norton, *The One Year Book of Hymns* (Wheaton, IL: Tyndale House Publishers Inc.), May 5.

Chapter 2

Divine Love

"Worship is all that we are, responding to all that He is." John MacArthur[6]

Did you hear about the computer technician who got a call from an angry customer whose computer kept telling him he was "bad and invalid?"

The technician explained, "No, not you sir. The message is telling you the command you entered was "bad and invalid."

All I can say is that customer must have had a guilty conscience because his protest sheds light on a real problem. For it is written, "There is no one righteous, not even one; there is no one who understands, no one who seeks God. All have turned away, they have together become worthless; there is no one who does good, not even one" (Rom 3:10-12).

For those of us who are self-reliant this is a crushing thought. Unless we learn to walk with God, though Christ, we are all "bad and invalid."

Have you noticed that the world disagrees with this? I think it's because people want to look to themselves for fulfillment instead of looking to God.

But contrary to the teachings of psychology professor Abraham Maslow, who taught in his famous Hierarchy of Needs theorem, the individual's highest human need is for "self-actualization," I believe that finding complete fulfillment in one's self is nothing more than a delusion. You

---

[6] John MacArthur, *True Worship; Study Notes, Selected Scriptures* (Word of Grace Communications, Panorama City, CA: 1982), P. 80.

see, God created us to be complete only in him. So, to deny God is to deny yourself fulfillment as well as forgiveness. Therefore, our highest need then is not for self-actualization but for God-actualization. The best way to find God-actualization is seeking God through the forgiveness provided by Jesus, then living a life that acknowledges and worships God.

But when I say *worship*, I'm not talking about the singing of songs like *Holy, Holy, Holy* or *Amazing Grace*, though singing hymns and songs of praise is certainly a wonderful form of worship. What I'm focusing on is *lifestyle* worship; learning how to live a life that acknowledges God with the love, respect, and thanks he deserves. Though lifestyle worship is the key to a deeper relationship with God, it's meaningless unless we learn to worship in love, a love which reflects the love he first gave to us. 1 John 4:19 says, "We love because he first loved us."

The Wrong Turn

I'm now re-queuing the story of Cain and Able, the story of two brothers who sought to pay honor to God. How did a quest to honor God lead to murder? Let's press play to find out...

...There's handsome, young Able. As a show of his love and devotion to God, he's sacrificing the firstborn of his beloved lambs to God. God is pleased with his sacrifice because it cost Able something and proves his act of worship is from his heart.

But wait! Cain is relaxing in the shade. When it's his turn to pay honor to God, he meanders to his orchards and picks a few pomegranates and lays them on the stone altar.

Abel's gift came at an expense to self but Cain's gift came as a quick solution without cost to self. It's no wonder

God liked Abel's gift best. Here's the problem: God's pleasure with Abel triggered Cain's jealousy.

Listen as God tries to calm Cain, "Why are you angry? Why is your face downcast? If you do what is right, will you not be accepted? But if you do not do what is right, sin is crouching at your door; it desires to have you, but you must master it." (Gen 4:6-7)

Cain doesn't listen to God's warning and tries yet another shortcut when he coaxes his brother to go out to the far field with him. "Let's go out to the field."

If you're squeamish, shield your eyes as Cain kills his competition for God's favor by thrusting his blade into Abel's heart.

Watch as the Lord calls to Cain, "Where is your brother Abel?

"I don't know. Am I my brother's keeper?

"What have you done? Listen! Your brother's blood cries out to me from the ground (Gen 4:8-10).

We can see Cain's offering was born of laziness, which led to jealousy, then to pride, and finally to murder. This was a gift God did not count as worship.

We'll fast-forward our movie now, past Abraham, past Moses, and to a time when God was worshipped with animal sacrifices in the temple. We've landed in the book of Malachi where we soon discover there's a problem with the people's sacrifices to God. They are *tainted*. No longer do the priests or people care enough about God to give him their best. Instead, they're sacrificing lame and blind animals and the Lord had something to say about it. "Cursed is the cheat who has an acceptable male in his flock and vows to give it, but then sacrifices a blemished animal to the Lord. For I am a great king, and my name is to be feared among the nations (Malachi 1:14).

Notice the use of the word "cheat"? It comes from the Hebrew word *nakal* which means to defraud or to act treacherously.[7] In other words, the people were cheating or defrauding God as an act of worship, much like a husband would cheat his wife if he presented her with a bouquet of dead flowers from the neighbor's trash heap.

So let's put our movie on pause and discuss the best way to worship (or walk with) God.

Is Your Heart in the Right Place?

There is a difference between real and fake. A few years ago I bought a beautiful cubic zirconium ring set in fourteen karat gold for about two hundred dollars. It looked real. But it was a fake. One day I was in a jewelry shop and pulled off my ring and handed it to the jeweler and asked, "In your professional opinion, how much is this ring worth?"

His eyes widened and he pulled out his jeweler's glass and studied the stone. When he looked up he whispered in awe, "About twenty thousand dollars."

I grinned. "Really?"

Suddenly wise, the jeweler put his lens away and pulled out a thermometer and took the stone's temperature. He exclaimed, "This diamond is a fake."

"How do you know?"

"Because real diamonds are cold. This "diamond" is room temperature."

---

[7] Biblesoft's New Exhaustive Strong's Numbers and Concordance with Expanded Greek-Hebrew Dictionary. Copyright (c) 1994, Biblesoft and International Bible Translators, Inc.

This illustration puts a new meaning on what Jesus said to the church of Laodicea in Revelations 3:15-18, "I know your deeds, that you are neither cold nor hot. I wish you were either one or the other! So, because you are lukewarm-neither hot nor cold—I am about to spit you out of my mouth. You say, 'I am rich; I have acquired wealth and do not need a thing.' But you do not realize that you are wretched, pitiful, poor, blind and naked. I counsel you to buy from me gold refined in the fire, so you can become rich; and white clothes to wear, so you can cover your shameful nakedness; and salve to put on your eyes, so you can see."

Yhouzer!

The church of Laodicea is like a cubic zirconium. The church may look good, but in reality, its worship and deeds were faked. The people of Laodicea were *not* living a lifestyle of worship. Considering the worship of God no longer required animal sacrifices, how did these churchgoers manage to fail the test? I think they failed because their worship was no longer motivated by a deep love for God or a commitment to live for him.

It's as John MacArthur once said, "How tragic it is for the Christian who understands that he is called and redeemed to worship God, to not worship God as fully as he ought."[8]

Perhaps the problem is simply this; *we don't love God enough.*

So many believers today want to worship God just by going through the motions, and that often includes me. How many times have I stood in a worship service and pondered my next meal or how I'll spend my afternoon. In those times, I only attended God without worshipping him from my

---

[8] John MacArthur, P. 25.

heart. When my heart, mind, words, and actions don't match, I'm not truly worshipping God.

Let me fast-forward *The God You Need To Know* to this scene where Jesus and his disciples are picnicking beneath a tree. *Oh dear,* here come the religious leaders draped in their tasseled prayer shawls. See how they scowl at Jesus. The first leader strokes his gray beard as he watches the disciples eat their lunch. He folds his arms across his chest and demands of Jesus, "Why don't your disciples live according to the tradition of the elders instead of eating their food with 'unclean' hands?"

Jesus answered him, " Isaiah was right when he prophesied about you hypocrites; as it is written: 'These people honor me with their lips, but their hearts are far from me. They worship me in vain; their teachings are but rules taught by men.'

"You have let go of the commands of God and are holding on to the traditions of men. You have a fine way of setting aside the commands of God in order to observe your own traditions! For Moses said, 'Honor your father and your mother,' and, 'Anyone who curses his father or mother must be put to death.' But you say that if a man says to his father or mother: 'Whatever help you might otherwise have received from me is a gift devoted to God.' Then you no longer let him do anything for his father or mother. Thus you nullify the word of God by your tradition that you have handed down. And you do many things like that (Mark 7:5-13).

The leaders are shocked by Jesus' outburst and simply stare, their scowls deepening. For Jesus' message was loud and clear, *"You may look real but you're fake. You pretend to honor your mother and father, but you find loopholes so you won't have to be financially responsible for their care. That shows your true heart, you frauds!"*

Jesus turns to the crowd to clarify his rebuke of their religious leaders. "Listen to me, everyone, and understand this. Nothing outside a man can make him 'unclean' by going into him. Rather, it is what comes out of a man that makes him 'unclean'" (Mark 7:14-15).

Ask yourself the hard question, when it comes to loving God, what is your life saying about you? Are you going through the motions or is your love for God illustrated in how you live your life?

Respect God

I was watching a program about the world's greatest explosions when a bomb expert looked into the camera and said, "If you don't fear bombs, you don't respect them."

The same could be said about our relationship with God, "If you don't fear him, you don't respect him." Scripture for Psalms 111:10 backs up this idea, "The fear of the LORD is the beginning of wisdom."

God is not our great big buddy in the sky. Though he loves us, he's not our pet. He's powerful and mighty. Though he's forgiving, he can be provoked to anger. By his own admission he is *jealous*. Certainly he's not jealous of us, he's jealous for our attention. In fact, he's jealous of anything that pulls our allegiance from him. But I think the main problem is we not only under appreciate him, we fail to give him the respect and attention he deserves because we've lost sight of the fact that he is the *all powerful God*.

Check out what happened the night Jesus' disciples got awed by Jesus. I'll queue it up so you can see…

…There, the disciples are fishing out on the lake when the wind picks up. When they decide it's time to start back to shore, they see a man walking toward them—*on top of the water*. They cry out, "Look! A ghost!"

Jesus calls to them, "Take courage! It is I. Don't be afraid."

Peter calls back, "Lord, if it's you, tell me to come to you on the water."

"Come!"

With his eyes on Jesus, Peter jumps on top the rough sea and practically skips across the water to meet up with Jesus. Peter does great until he looks down at the waves rolling beneath his feet. As soon as Peter's eyes are off of Jesus, he sinks. "Lord, save me!"

Jesus takes him by the hand and lifts him up. "You of little faith, why did you doubt?"

As Peter and Jesus climb into the boat, the wind stops and the disciples bow down, right into the puddles at the bottom of the boat. (Matt 14:26-33)

They're in awe because they've encountered the power of Jesus. When we encounter the power of God, the same thing happens to us; we are filled with both fear and respect. It's like Kay Arthur says, "For if He is God, then He must be honored as God."[9]

Be Humble Before God

Jack Hayford, the founding pastor of the Church of the Way in Van Nuys, once said, "God's word indicates that He is not looking for something brilliant, but something broken: 'The sacrifices of God are a broken spirit; a broken and contrite heart, O God you will not despise'" (Ps 51:17).[10]

---

[9] Kay Arthur, P. 53.
[10] Jack Hayford quote, *Inside Out Worship; Insights for Passionate and Purposeful Worship*, Matt Redman,P. 90.

22

Remember the parable Jesus told about the tax collector? In the story he tells of two men who go to the temple to pray. One man was a Pharisee and the other man was a despised tax collector. The Pharisee stood proudly and prayed, "God, I thank you that I am not like other men-robbers, evildoers, adulterers-or even like this tax collector. I fast twice a week and give a tenth of all I get."

But the tax collector stood at a distance. He would not even look up to heaven, but beat his breast and said, "God, have mercy on me, a sinner."

Jesus explained, ""I tell you that this man, rather than the other, went home justified before God. For everyone who exalts himself will be humbled, and he who humbles himself will be exalted" (Luke 18:9-14).

Again, it's a pride thing. But the good news is worship is the opposite of pride.

Do Not Worship God For Self-Gain

We don't worship God for what we can get, we worship God for who he is. We worship him in both times of plenty and times of lack. I love this prayer found in Habakuk 3:17-18:

> *Though the fig tree does not bud*
> *and there are no grapes on the vines,*
> *though the olive crop fails*
> *and the fields produce no food,*
> *though there are no sheep in the pen*
> *and no cattle in the stalls,*
> *   yet I will rejoice in the LORD,*
> *I will be joyful in God my Savior.*
> (Reread this passage as a prayer.)

Worship God in Obedience

God is calling to us because he wants more of us. He wants our heart, our love, our devotion, and our service. He wants our obedience.

> *Who may ascend the hill of the LORD?*
> *Who may stand in his holy place?*
> *He who has clean hands and a pure heart,*
> *who does not lift up his soul to an idol*
> *or swear by what is false.*
> *He will receive blessing from the LORD*
> *and vindication from God his Savior.*
> *Such is the generation of those who seek him,*
> *who seek your face, O God of Jacob* (Ps 24:3-6).

A person with clean hands is a person who obeys the Lord. A person with a pure heart is a person who has been renewed by the power of God. That person is not simply going through the motions just to look good; that person is serving God through the love in his or her heart.

A Person Who Worships God - Give's God Ownership

My brother gave me a CD of a talk given by Otto Koning, a former missionary to New Guinea. Otto's story about his pineapple garden changed my perspective on why we should give God ownership of the details in our lives.

It seems Otto waited three years for his pineapple plants to mature enough to produce fruit. But to Otto's chagrin, the natives stole the pineapples even before they were ripe and that's how Otto became known as an angry white man.

Year after year, Otto tried to persuade the people to stop stealing his pineapples. He even tried closing both the clinic and the store he ran in an effort to persuade the villagers to stop stealing. But the closures only caused the people he was trying to serve to move away.

Finally, Otto gave *his rights* to the pineapples to God, thinking his "sacrifice" would be the key in finally winning a juicy pineapple of his own. When thieves continued to steal the pineapple, Otto continued his tantrums. Finally, in desperation, Otto *gave* the pineapple garden to God. In so doing, he finally found freedom from the anger that consumed him. Soon he'd even wave at the thieves who frequented his garden. One day, one of the men from the tribe asked, "You've changed. Did you finally become a Christian?"

This comment devastated Otto. He humbly replied, "Yes, I have become a Christian."

"But why don't you get angry when we steal your pineapples?"

"I gave the pineapples away."

The next morning, at sunrise, the entire tribe stood at Otto's front door.

The chief said, "We must know who owns the pineapples."

"I gave the garden to God," the missionary said.

The chief was alarmed. "Your God is very powerful and can see in the dark?"

"Yes," Otto said.

"Then you must take the garden back from God."

"I can't."

"How long ago did you give the garden to God?" the chief asked.

"About six months ago."

The tribe was furious. As it turned out, for the past six months, the tribe had been plagued with trouble. The women weren't getting pregnant. The hunters weren't bringing home wild boars. They had long tried to determine who had brought this trouble into their camp. Now they knew. They had been stealing pineapples from God.

The situation was tense until one of the warriors stood up for Otto. "Don't you see he wants to be a Christian?"

Otto said, "Please let me be a Christian."

The chief finally agreed.

Afterward, most of the natives stopped stealing the fruit and prosperity came back to the tribe. Not only did Otto get to eat some of the pineapple crop, the members of the tribe became followers of Christ.

Otto summed up his adventures with this statement. "God took care of his fruit so much better than I could."[11]

Did you notice when Otto gave his garden to God, God brought an even greater harvest? A harvest of souls.

Could it be that Otto's focus on the pineapple had been akin to his worship of pineapple? When Otto gave his focus to God, God gave Otto the harvest.

When God is not the focus of our lives, what we focus on becomes what we worship.

Perhaps like Otto, if we want to join God's living story, we need to not only give up the rights to the things we think we control, we need to give God ownership. That way our hearts will not be confused as to whom we worship and our lives will produce fruit that will last.

---

[11] Adapted from recorded testimony of former New Guinea missionary, Otto Koning as well as The Pineapple Story, (Oak Brook, IL: Institute in Basic Life Principles, Inc., 1978), www.Iblp.org.

Love Notes:

In this chapter, we can surmise that to join God's living story, we have to worship from our hearts in the following ways:

- Turn our hearts toward God.

- Be careful to give God our very best, not our cast offs.

- Develop a deeper respect for God.

- Humble ourselves before God.

- Worship to give to God, not to get from God.

- Give God ownership of what we value most.

- Place God above the things we value.

Worship Experience:

Experience One:

If anything, we've learned this; what we focus on is what we worship and the more we focus on God, the more our hearts will worship him.

Let's look at how the early church worshipped God. Evaluate which of these practices you could incorporate into your own walk with God:

- Prayer

- Eating together (with other Christians)

- Confession of sins

- Reading the scriptures

- Preaching

- Singing

- Giving to the poor

- Taking a collection/or giving

- Public confession of faith

- Greeting (other believers) with a holy kiss (or showing other forms of affectionate greetings like handshakes or hugs.)

- Partaking of the Lord's Supper

- Giving Thanks

- Using spiritual gifts.[12]

Experience Two:

Let's take some time to worship through continued study of God's names...

- **El Shaddai** (el shaw-DIE) – One of God's names meaning "all sufficient one of blessings" and is also used in Genesis 17:1-2, "When Abram was ninety-nine years old, the LORD appeared to him and said, "I am God Almighty (El Shaddai); walk before me and be blameless. I will confirm my covenant between me and you and will greatly increase your numbers."[13]

  Praise: El Shaddai, you are the God Almighty, the source of my every blessing. You are the all-sufficient one, the God of the mountains, the God of my heart. I give you honor and glory and thanksgiving for all you have done for me. You are so great, so mighty, so sufficient. You are the all in all, my everything.

- **El Elyon** (el yuhn) – One of God's names meaning "God most high." It's also used in Psalms 78:35

12 Adapted from *Inside Out Worship; Insights for Passionate and Purposeful Worship,* P. 86 –87.
13 *The Names of God* Wall Chart.

"They remembered that God (El Elyon) was their Rock, that God Most High was their Redeemer."[14]

Praise: El Elyon, God Most High, help me to remember that you are my rock and my redeemer. You are the Lord most high, there is no other name higher than yours. You are higher than the mountains, and even higher than the universe, for you created the mountains and the universe. I pay you honor as I think of you and you eternal greatness. You are my God.

Experience Three:

The following is a praise song that you can sing, speak or whisper in your heart to God. It's a hymn of worship that demonstrates how the person who is motivated by God's love, lives his life as an act of worship.

Take Time to be Holy

Take time to be holy,
Speak oft with thy Lord;
Abide in Him always,
And feed on His Word.
Make friends of God's children;
Help those who are weak;
Forgetting in nothing
His blessing to seek.

---

[14] Ibid.

Take time to be holy,
The world rushes on;
Much time spend in secret
With Jesus alone;
By looking to Jesus,
Like Him thou shalt be;
Thy friends in thy conduct
His likeness shall see.

Take time to be holy,
Let Him be thy guide,
And run not before Him
Whatever betide;
In joy or in sorrow
Still follow the Lord,
And, looking to Jesus,
Still trust in His Word.

Take time to be holy,
Be calm in thy soul;
Each thought and each motive
Beneath His control;
Thus led by His Spirit
To fountains of love,
Thou soon shalt be fitted
For service above.

William Dunn Longstaff (1822-1894)[15]

---

[15] Take Time to Be Holy by William Dunn Longstaff , (Baxter Station, Louisville, KY: *Great Songs of the Church Number Two*, E.L. Jorgenson Compiler, Edition of 1944, Great Songs Press) P. 503.

Chapter 3

Divine Trust

"The heart of God loves a persevering worshipper, who though overwhelmed by many troubles, is overwhelmed even more by the beauty of God." – Matt Redman[16]

It's a Trust Thing

No matter where I go, I meet brokenhearted people. They tell me their life stories:

My husband betrayed me.

My granddaughter committed suicide.

My sister died in a natural disaster.

My son is on drugs.

My mother made me have an abortion.

My brother died of cancer.

I have a terrible disease.

I was molested.

My husband abuses me.

My wife and I lost our baby.

And the list goes on. In fact, I think more people today carry more grief and heartache than ever before. And they're counting it all as rejection from God.

A young woman told me, "I'm a failure. My Christian walk is not working. I know because God isn't answering

---

[16] Matt Redman, *The Unquenchable Worshipper, Coming Back to the Heart of Worship,* (Ventura, CA: Regal Books from Gospel Light, 2001), P. 25.

my prayers and that means he doesn't love me. I might as well be dead."

Wait a minute. *Whoever said life would never hurt?*

Yes, bad things happen. Some of these difficulties are caused by our own actions or the actions of others, or even the acts of nature or by what may seem like random bad luck. The causes may vary, but in all this trouble, in all this pain, God has not forgotten us and he loves us with an everlasting love.

But we're left with the question – *why doesn't God always come to our rescue?*

We've heard it said, "And we know that in all things God works for the good of those who love him, who have been called according to his purpose." (Romans 8:28) How could this Scripture possibly be true in all of our difficulties and situations?

Let me tell you a story…

My friend told me that every spring the wrens try to build nests under the eaves of her house. But every morning she and her son sweep the nests down. Why? It's a *dog* thing. It seems their dogs have a taste for baby birds.

My friend sweeps down the nests as an act of love and concern. But the birds don't seem to understand. Every morning, during nesting season, my friend and her son find bright yellow blades of grass in every eave. Jackie theorizes the birds are testing to see which of their construction sites will remain undisturbed. It hurts, but Jackie and her son continue to sweep out the blades of grass until the birds build their nests elsewhere.

If the birds could talk about my friend and her son, do you think they'd say, "Thank goodness for these two people who are looking out for us?" Or, "Don't they care what happens to us? Don't they want us to raise our families in peace?"

Perhaps you've had a few plans swept away and you've wondered, "Where is God? Doesn't he love me? Why isn't he looking out for me?" Perhaps he is looking out for you, protecting you from dangers you don't understand. Well that certainly explains some circumstances, but not all.

Do you understand all that is in the heart and the mind of God? Were you there when he created the dawn? Do you understand all the mysteries of the atom? Do you know how he slung the stars into place? Then how do you know he's not working for the good?

Let's explore a hypothetical situation by pretending your son has a drinking problem and gets picked up for driving drunk.

You'd like to see him avoid losing his driver's license; I mean how's he going to get to work unless you drive him? So you pray and ask God to perform a miracle. But the judge throws the book at him. Not only does your son lose his license, he's to serve some jail time.

How could God allow this, especially considering this is not what you prayed?

But what if this is God's way of giving your son the miracle of a second chance; a wakeup call that leads to sobriety and turns his heart to God? What if it wasn't God who failed your son, but your original prayer? What if God said 'no' to your prayer in order to work all things for the good in your son's behalf? Would you be willing to walk through the difficulty to get to the best result? Would you be willing to walk with a grateful heart even if you didn't understand God's intent? Okay, I know some situations are even more complicated than the hypothetical one I described. But does that mean we can't trust God?

When Job, a righteous man who loved God, faced calamities that seemed useless, he said; "Though he slay me, yet will I hope in him" (Job 13:15).

I looked up this passage in the Barnes Notes electronic commentary and found this bit of discussion, "[Yet will I trust in him] The word used here *yaachal* means properly to wait, stay, delay; and it usually conveys the idea of waiting on one with an expectation of aid or help. Hence, it means to hope. The sense here is, that his expectation or hope was in God…it implies that even in death, or after death, he would confide in God. He would adhere to him, and would still feel that beyond death he would bless him."[17]

Beyond death?

Could it be that our perspective of our life, our times and our troubles are too limited? Could God be using even the most difficult circumstances to work out things "for the good" even in the life to come?

My mind is too small to comprehend and to explain these mysteries. But here's what I can comprehend. I can trust God, no matter what. We walk with God, not for what we'll get, but because of who he is. Author Marva Dawn, in her book, *A Royal "Waste" of Time: The Splendor of Worshiping God and Being Church for the World* says, "The entire reason for our worship is that God deserves it. Moreover, it isn't even useful for earning points with God, for what we do in worship won't change one whit how God feels about us. We will always still be helpless sinners caught in our endless inability to be what we should be or to make ourselves better – and God will always still be merciful, compassionate, and

---

[17] Biblesoft's New Exhaustive Strong's Numbers and Concordance with Expanded Greek-Hebrew Dictionary.

gracious, abounding in steadfast love and ready to forgive us as we come to him."[18]

Walking in Worship

After a massive computer crash, I had to reconstruct my comprehensive outline for this book from my original research. I tried to start the process of putting the pieces back together but I felt confused. I just couldn't get organized until I tuned into a Christian radio station. The worship music seemed to act as a shield against the spirit of confusion that swallowed me. I suddenly knew how to start the reconstruction process. Not only that, but I was no longer upset about the loss of my files. I was enjoying reviewing my research. Plus, with a background of praise music, I could feel my spirit worship as the pieces fell back into place even better than before.

I'd experienced a direct result of what I call walking in no-matter-what-trust. It's the payoff of joy when you walk with God, regardless the circumstances.

Walking in No-Matter-What-Trust

It's time to show another clip from *The God You Need To Know*.

We're going to watch one of God's favorite men face a dilemma requiring him to walk in no-matter-what-trust. Give me a second to queue it up.

Ah, there's Abraham. Notice Abraham and his wife Sarah look old enough to be great-grandparents, yet there they are holding a newborn baby. Yep, that's their son, little Isaac, a child of God's promise. You see God promised both Abraham and Sarah they would be the mother and father of

---

[18] Marva Dawn, *A Royal "Waste" of Time: The Splendor of Worshiping God and Being Church for the World* (Grand Rapids, MI: Wm. B. Eerdmans Publishing Co., 1999), P.1.

a great nation. When they'd first heard this promise, both Abraham and Sarah chuckled. *Didn't God know they were both old AND childless?*

But the laugh was on them because some years later, as God had promised, Sarah gave birth to Isaac. After decades of waiting, God's promise came true.

I'm going to fast-forward a few years. See old Abraham smile as he sits under a tree watching his beloved son Isaac at play. If you listen in you'll hear God speak to him.

"Abraham!"

Abraham recognizes God's voice. "Here I am."

"Take your son, your only son, Isaac, whom you love, and go to the region of Moriah. Sacrifice him there as a burnt offering on one of the mountains I will tell you about."

Freeze the frame!

How could God ask Abraham to sacrifice this child of promise?

But watch what this old man does next. He gathers the dry wood and throws it across the back of his mule. He sticks his knife into his belt, grabs a stick of fire, then takes his little son's hand. Together they walk to the place God directed. Along the way, Isaac being a smart lad, realizes the sacrificial lamb is missing. Listen in as he turns his bright face to his father.

"Father?"

"Yes, my son?"

"The fire and wood are here, but where is the lamb for the burnt offering?"

"God himself will provide the lamb for the burnt offering, my son."

When they reach the place God told him about, Abraham gathers a few stones and builds an altar. He arranges the firewood then binds rope around his son. With tears running down his cheeks, Abraham places Isaac on the altar and lifts his knife, ready to plunge the blade into his only son.

The Angel of the Lord calls out, "Abraham! Abraham!"

"Here I am."

"Do not lay a hand on the boy. Do not do anything to him. Now I know that you fear God because you have not withheld from me your son, your only son."

Just past the altar, Abraham sees a ram caught by its horns in the thicket to sacrifice in place of his son. Abraham called that place The LORD Will Provide. To this day it is said, "On the mountain of the LORD it will be provided." (Gen 22:1-14)

I think God tested Abraham for the same reason professors test their students; to see what they know. God wants to know if we really know him enough to trust him.

I've read this story about Abraham and Isaac thousands of times and I thought I understood it. But that was before I lived it.

If you know my story, you know the person who's given me both the greatest difficulties and joys is my disabled daughter, Laura. When she was only eighteen-months-old she was injured in a violent car crash and spent a year in coma before waking up to a life of disability. God taught me so much from her precious life, and I admit it. I simply love and adore my sweet and innocent child, despite her handicaps.

A few years ago, one early December morning, I lay in bed as the sun cast its first glow into the chill of morning. I find these quiet moments the best time to listen for God's voice. In the quiet of my heart I prayed, "Lord, I love you. Do you have anything you want to tell me today?"

I felt his spirit stir within me and his still voice spoke in my inner ear. "There is a great difficulty you must face."

I sat up in bed and bowed my head. In my heart I whispered, "Tell me Lord. What is it you want me to know?"

"Laura will soon die."

I sat stunned, unable to whisper a prayer for several moments. I opened my eyes and stared into the dim light. "Oh Lord, I must take time to think about your words."

I spent the morning sitting beside Laura's bed, thinking what a special gift she'd been in my life. I thought of the joy she'd brought into our home, the total trust and patience she placed with her family and caregivers. What an example she'd been to so many. I held her hand and fought back tears as I cooed, "I love you, Laura."

I wondered, *If the Lord is bringing my daughter to himself, how will I cope with her absence? How will I go on?*

I thought of all the pain of Laura's original car accident so many years earlier. There had been the death of a dream, but no funeral. Would all that original grief wash over me when the Lord finally took my baby home? Would I have anything left to give to those to whom I ministered?

As I held Laura's hand, I spoke to the Lord. "I don't want you to take my daughter Lord; however, she belongs to you. I would never prevent her from coming home to you. How could I stand in her way?"

Then the Lord spoke to me again. He said, "Like Jacob with his son Isaac, I will not take Laura from you."

How I rejoiced, thanking the Lord for his gift of grace.

I soon forgot this experience with the Lord until early Christmas morning. It was 2:10 am and my husband and I were sound asleep when the house-wide alarm sounded.

We bolted to Laura's bedroom and saw a horrific sight. The ventilator rhythmically pumped air into Laura's lungs so she could breathe, but her chest did not move.

"Help me," the caregiver said. "Ambu bag Laura so I can try to figure out what's wrong with her vent."

I fitted the ambu bag on Laura's trach site, a small tube opening at the base of her neck. The blue bag looked like a balloon made of sturdy plastic. When squeezed, it's supposed to deliver a life saving breath. But no matter how hard I squeezed, Laura's chest did not rise and fall. In all her eighteen years of being on a vent, this had never happened before. Laura's skin darkened into a dusky blue as her lips turned purple. "Breathe, Laura breathe," I shouted to her.

Nothing.

Not today. Not Christmas Day, I thought as I realized we were losing her.

Her eyes filled with fear.

"Breathe Laura, breathe!" I called, "Jesus help us! Show us what to do!"

Laura's coloring continued to darken. My helper pulled off the ambu bag and rehooked Laura to her vent. The swoosh of a life saving breath was delivered, but Laura's chest did not rise.

Then I noticed. The light in Laura's eyes had dimmed.

We pulled the vent tubing off of Laura's track and tried to ambu bag her again.

The time was now 2:20 a.m. Laura had not shown any response in the past ten minutes. How long can a person live without air? I wondered, four minutes?

Laura's eyes were now so dark they looked as if they'd been switched off.

I pounded on Laura's chest, willing it to rise and fall. Nothing.

My helper quietly said. "It's time to call for help."

Because, I realized, *Laura is dead.*

My husband dialed 9-1-1.

At 2:35 a.m., over twenty-five minutes since Laura had taken a breath, the paramedics ran into my daughter's room and pulled our ambu bag off of her and replaced it with their own. They did nothing other than what we'd already done.

One paramedic asked me. "How long has your daughter been on a vent?"

"Eighteen years — tomorrow."

I gasped, and then silently prayed. "Lord, you said you weren't taking Laura but now she's dead. Did I misunderstand you? Would you take her on Christmas Day, a day short of the eighteen years since her accident?"

I ran to my room to grab a pair of jeans and a jacket. I would go to the hospital with Laura where they would pronounce her DOA.

In the privacy of my bedroom I cried out. "Lord, Laura is yours." I tried to focus on God. "Lord, I do not worship my daughter, I worship you. I trust you with Laura's life and with mine."

When I ran out of the bedroom, the paramedics had Laura on a stretcher and were ambu bagging her as they hurried to load her onto the ambulance.

I followed behind the ambulance in the van and parked outside the ER. But when I watched the team unload Laura I saw something amazing. Color had returned to Laura's cheeks.

Could it be?

When we rushed her into the ER, I knew it was true. Laura's spirit had returned to her body.

My diagnosis was soon confirmed by the medial team. Laura was alive!

When the medical team left the room, I quietly told the Lord, "I saw Laura was dead."

In his sweet, still voice, he spoke to my heart. "I told you she would die."

"But you sent her back."

"I said I would not take her from you, not yet. It's not her time. You have shown me you do not worship your daughter. You worship me. You trust me. This is exactly the place you need to be."

"Thank you Lord," I prayed. "Thank you, thank you, thank you."

Suddenly, Laura burped, then she laughed as if she thought her burp was the funniest thing in the world.

Then I knew, despite the events of the evening, not only was Laura alive, she was still the girl she had been when I had kissed her goodnight and tucked her into her bed only hours before.

We were back home by five a.m., tucking Laura back into her bed as we sang the Hallelujah Chorus with the Christmas music on the radio, still praising God for bringing Laura back from the dead.

What was the moment Laura returned to her body? I can't help but believe it was the moment I let go and gave God permission to take her home.

Someday the Lord will take my precious daughter to heaven and when he does, I will cry bitterly, I may even feel deep despair. But through my pain and grief I will know Laura is in a better place. Her sweet innocent spirit will be intact, but her broken, disabled body will be restored.

But for now, God has left her with me and I rejoice.

Somehow, like Abraham, I feel as though I've passed a test. I will worship God, whatever happens. I will trust him and know that all things work for the good.

If you find yourself in a place where you need to walk in no-matter-what-trust, think on Psalms 105:4, "Look to the LORD and his strength; seek his face always."

That's the key. We need to look at God, not the circumstance.

Look at God, not the Circumstance

We can trust God when we quit looking at our own circumstances and focus on his beauty. A. Z. Tozer once said, "What the church needs today is a restoration of the vision of the Most High God."[19] This is absolutely true. When we get a divine revelation of God, we cannot help but walk in trust.

---

[19] A.Z. Tozer, *Worship and Entertainment,* (Camp Hill, PA: Christian Publications, 1998) p. 54.

I recently enjoyed *The Worship Series* by Matt Redman. In his book, *Facedown*, he created a wonderful description of God I'd like to share.

"The God we worship is clothed in mystery. He reveals and He conceals. He invites and He hides. He confounds and He confides. The God who rests but never sleeps. Who thunders and whispers, terrifies and befriends. Whose anger lasts only a moment, but whose favor lasts a lifetime. Who is all consuming yet kind, all knowing but capable of forgetting the sins he forgives. The God who wounds and bounds up, who injures and who heals. The King whose footstool is the earth, yet humbly washed the earth from the feet of those he discipled. Who reigns in righteousness yet carried our shamefulness. Who walked in the Garden of Eden in the cool of the day, yet sweated drops of blood in the Garden of Gethsemane one agonizing night...

"The suffering servant. The sinless friend of sinners. The Savior who hung in agony on beams of wood he Himself had called into being. He is fearless yet welcoming, unfathomable yet knowable. The God of kings and beggars, presidents and paupers. Who fathers the fatherless and works through our weakness. Burning with holiness yet refreshingly graceful.

"He who is worshipped by the multitudes of heaven yet rejoices over a single returning heart. Perfect in every way yet able to help those who are being tempted. He is faithful even to the faithless, for he cannot disown Himself. This is the God we worship – the God of all mystery."[20]

---

[20] Matt Redman, *Facedown*, (Ventura, CA: Regal Books from Gospel Light, 2001),

What a marvelous description. Yet, it's only a tiny glimpse at the majesty of God. For God is so much more lovely and wonderful and powerful and holy than anyone can adequately put into words. Still, if we can try to imagine how majestic God is, our difficulties will pale in the light of his glory.

How to Walk with God when You're in the Belly of the Whale

I've just queued up another segment of *The God You Need To Know* (several hundred years past the story of Abraham and Isaac.)

Meet the prophet Jonah. Jonah was a man with a message from God, a message he didn't want to deliver. You see God called him to go to the city of Nineveh to tell the people if they didn't repent, they would be destroyed. Problem? Jonah hated this message about as much as he hated the people of Nineveh.

Look there, he's down at the docks in Joppa, taking passage on a boat headed for Tarshish. Isn't Tarshish in the wrong direction? Sure is. It looks like he's getting away with running from God. But then, maybe I spoke too soon. Although we can see that Jonah's below deck taking a little snooze, we also see his boat is caught in a dangerous squall.

The captain shakes Jonah awake, "How can you sleep? Get up and call on your god! Maybe he will take notice of us, and we will not perish."

Jonah pokes his head out from the hold in time to see lightening flash across the sky as the waves turn into monstrous, gray swells. A look of guilt spreads across Jonah's face. They are in serious trouble and he knows why.

P. 37-38.

1

1

A group of sailors try to hold on to the railing as they cast their cargo overboard. One says, "Come, let us cast lots to find out who is responsible for this calamity."

Is there any surprise the lot falls to Jonah?

The sailors turn to the prophet and demand answers. "What do you do? Where do you come from? What is your country? From what people are you?"

Jonah answers, "I am a Hebrew and I worship the LORD, the God of heaven, who made the sea and the land."

The sailors look from one to another and their eyes widen. Jonah serves a God they fear. As the thunder booms, their ship falls then lifts as another swell almost capsizes them.

The sailors grab on to whatever's nailed down as another wave washes across the deck. One sailor shouts above the wind, "What have you done? What should we do to you to make the sea calm down for us?"

Jonah doesn't hide his guilt. He simply says, "Pick me up and throw me into the sea, and it will become calm. I know that it is my fault that this great storm has come upon you."

Bless their hearts. The sailors won't hear of it. They fight the waves with all their strength but the storm simply overpowers them. Finally, they fall on their knees before God, "O LORD, please do not let us die for taking this man's life. Do not hold us accountable for killing an innocent man, for you, O LORD, have done as you pleased."

They then grab Jonah and with a mighty heave, they toss him into the raging sea. The sea calms and they sail into peaceful waters, leaving Jonah bobbing on the waves, a long way from shore.

You might say Jonah's in hot water. As if to prove the point, the Lord sends a great fish to swallow him. (Jonah 1:5-2:1)

This is where the screen goes dark. There's not much to see in the belly of a whale and there's not much to do there either, except pray. I'll turn up the audio so you can hear what Jonah says to God.

> "In my distress I called to the LORD, and he answered me. From the depths of the grave I called for help, and you listened to my cry. You hurled me into the deep, into the very heart of the seas, and the currents swirled about me; all your waves and breakers swept over me. I said, 'I have been banished from your sight; yet I will look again toward your holy temple.' The engulfing waters threatened me, the deep surrounded me; seaweed was wrapped around my head. To the roots of the mountains I sank down; the earth beneath barred me in forever. But you brought my life up from the pit, O LORD my God.
>
> "When my life was ebbing away, I remembered you, LORD, and my prayer rose to you, to your holy temple.
>
> "Those who cling to worthless idols forfeit the grace that could be theirs. But I, with a song of thanksgiving, will sacrifice to you. What I have vowed I will make good. Salvation comes from the LORD" (Jonah 2:2-9).

God heard Jonah's prayer because after three days the whale vomits Jonah near the beach. (I'm glad this production doesn't come with smell effects.) There he is, wrapped in seaweed and bleached white by the whale's gastric juices. He crawls out of the waves and sinks his knees into the sand, thanking God for delivering him.

Instead of running away, this time Jonah heads to Nineveh where he gives the people a message from God.

The people believe Jonah and turn from their sins. And though—or maybe even because—Jonah smelled a bit fishy, his mission was quickly accomplished.

Whether or not you've disobeyed God, as Jonah did when he sailed away from God's plan, or whether you've separated yourself from God due to sin, anger, or bitterness, you may have found yourself in a whale of trouble. If so, turn your private prison into your sanctuary of prayer and brokenness before God. God may still cause your circumstances to spit you out. But no matter, you need to walk with God wherever he wants to take you, even if it's to Nineveh.

Walking in Acceptance:

John MacArthur says, "The worship of acceptance is to be willing to accept your circumstances—your place in life, your job, your career, your partner, your children—and be willing to say, 'God, You know all of the things that are happening to me (the loss of your loved one, the loss of your child, the loss of your job, the pain of illness), and yet in the midst of it all, I will worship You.'"[21]

Of course, even when you accept your circumstances you're still allowed to pray and continue to seek God to change them. But the key is you walk with him regardless of how he answers.

I was speaking at a conference when a young mother approached. She told me her little girl asked her why God put her in a wheelchair. She asked me, "What should I say?"

"Tell her though her life isn't easy, God is with her. I can imagine God pointing her out to his angels. 'Do you see this little one? See how, despite her hardships and handicaps she trusts in me? But compare her to that other one I've graced

---

[21] John MacArthur, P. 100.

with the ability to win gold medals. Despite all she's been given, she chooses to ignore me. But this little one in a wheelchair, she walks with me.'"

In the end, it's not what you can do. It's whom you walk with.

The Potter Knows Best

For can the potter not do with you as he wants?

Wendy Lawton, in her book, *Impressions in Clay*, describes the potter at work. She says, "The potter may squash the clay many times during the creative process. Sometimes the potential vessel comes up an inch or two before a flaw develops and the potter presses it back to the wheel. Other times he will draw it all the way up to a lip, and seeing a wobble, take it back down. The wheel continues to rotate throughout the up-and-down process, until the pot is complete." Wendy compared this process to our spiritual journey, she says, "How often do we begin to rise off the wheel, only to be thumped back down? The Potter is in control, and the rising and lowering of the clay is part of the process."[22]

Will you accept the fact the potter is at work, that you can trust him, and that you can walk with him no matter what?

Love Notes:

In this chapter we've discovered:

- Difficult circumstances do not mean God doesn't love us.

- Our perspective regarding our circumstances is not always the same as God's perspective.

---

[22] Wendy Lawton, *Impressions in Clay*, (Chicago, IL: Moody Publishers, 2005), P. 68.

- Sometimes we have to press into and through our circumstances before we see God's divine plan.

- God tests us to see if we trust him.

- Our problems pale in the light of his glory.

- It's all about walking with God.

- We can always come to God with requests, however we should walk with him no matter how he answers them.

A Power Walk Experience:

"All worship is a response to a revelation – it's only as we breathe in more of the wonder of God that we can breathe out a fuller response to Him." – Matt Redman[23]

Experience One:

Reread Jonah's prayer, and pray it as your own.

Experience Two:

Contemplate on this name of God.

- Jehovah-Jireh (juh-HO-vah JI-rah) – One use of this name is found in Gen 22:13-14 meaning, "the Lord will provide." It was used to describe God as he provided a sacrificial ram to use in the place of Abraham's son, Isaac. "Abraham looked up and there in a thicket he saw a ram caught by its horns. He went over and took the ram and sacrificed it as a burnt offering instead of his son. So Abraham called that place The LORD Will Provide (Jehovah-Jireh). And to this day it is said, 'On the mountain of the LORD it will be provided.'"[24]

---

[23] Matt Redman, P. 96.
[24] *The Names of God* Wall Chart.

Pray:

Jehovah-Jireh, you are the Lord who will provide in all my circumstances. You provided for Abraham by sending him a sacrificial ram to use instead of his own son, Isaac. You provided a sacrifice, your own son, to be used as a sacrifice in place of me. How can I say thank you for such a gift of love? I in no way deserved it. Yet you freely give me this gift so I can worship and walk with you. I bow down to you, o Holy One.

Chapter 4

Divine Obedience

If worship doesn't propel you into greater obedience, call it what you will, but it isn't worship. – John MacAuthur[25]

In an episode of the TV medial drama, House MD, a world-class bicyclist named Jeff Hastert (Kristoffer Polaha), is rushed to the hospital after respiratory arrest. While in ICU, Jeff, thanks his doctors for staying late. Dr. Foremen (Omar Epps) accepts his thanks but Dr. Cameron (Jennifer Morrison) is clearly angry as she suspects Jeff's been cheating in his bike races by blood doping. She sarcastically asks him if he *likes* being a hero.

When he replies, "It's a living," Dr. Cameron wants to know if he feels any sense of responsibility to the kids who worship him.

So Jeff tells the doctor about getting a letter from a guy who wanted him to send a note to his son because the son worshipped him. "Do you know what worship means? I looked it up. It means to love. Unquestionably. Uncritically. So the kid doesn't even know me but he loves me. Unquestionably. Uncritically." The scene ends as this human object of worship goes into convulsions.[26] But the point is made. Worship is an act of focus, love and adoration.

With this definition of worship in mind, it's easy to see that everyone *worships* someone or something. The question each of us must ask is who or what do we worship?

---

25 John MacArthur, P. 6.
26 Quotes from Fox's House MD, aired 11/15/06, episode titled "Spin" (2005) staring Hugh Laurie, Lisa Edelstein, Omar Epps.

John MacAuthur said, "Every religion that does not rightly discern God, worships a false god. Every materialist, every irreligious atheist, and every agnostic who wouldn't even darken the door of religion, worships some material god of his own invention. Even if it's himself. It's all unacceptable to God...it damns the soul."[27]

In the book, *The Air I Breathe*, Louie Giglio says, "You may not consider yourself a "worshiping" kind of person, but you cannot help but worship... something. It's what you were made to do.

"Should you for some reason choose not to give God what He desires, you'll worship anyway – simply exchanging the Creator for something He has created.

"Think of it this way: Worship is simply about value. The simplest definition I can give is this; Worship is our response to what we value most...."That 'thing' might be a relationship. A dream. A position. Status. Something you own. A name. A job. Some kind of pleasure. Whatever name you put on it, this 'thing' is what you've concluded in your heart is worth most to you. And whatever is worth most to you is—you guessed it—what you worship.

"Worship in essence, is declaring what we value most. As a result, worship fuels our actions, becoming the driving force in all we do."[28]

Some of the more common gods worshipped by our culture include:

- **Sex** – When you worship sex, it enslaves, degrades, ruins reputation, and can lead to disease, and the sacrifice of human beings through abortion.

---

[27] John MacArthur, P. 11.
[28] Louie Giglio, *The Air I Breathe* (Sisters, OR: Multnomah Publishers Inc., 2003), P. 1.

- **Money** – When you worship money, you sell yourself short of a deeper relationship with God. Money buys the enslavement of your will to greed. Greed can cause you to commit wrongs, trample others, and to spend your soul on that which is not eternal.

- **Pride** – When you worship pride, you worship and serve yourself. To worship God, you must humble yourself before God and serve *him*.

Notice that each false god, like sex, money or pride, has the power to enslave, demand sacrifice as well as your allegiance. You have no choice, you will be enslaved to that which you worship. Dr. Erwin W. Lutzer says, "There is a world of difference between being a slave to the True God and a slave to an idol because when you become a slave to an idol you become a slave to sin."[29]

Do you worship anyone or anything beside Jehovah, the LORD of the universe? Perhaps you should take inventory of what you value most and what captures your focus. In that light, you might be surprised to see exactly what and who it is you worship.

I know I was.

I'd been feeling stressed out. My nonprofit organization, Right to the Heart Ministries, had met much success; ministering to almost a million people in two years and seeing well over 200,000 people come to faith.

But our Internet work came with a large price tag. That spring, we'd lost two major supporters who'd decided to

[29] Dr. Erwin W. Lutzer quote from *The Running to Win* radio program, "In Competition With God, Part 3" Friday, June 22, 2006, www.OnePlace.com, © 2006, Oneplace.com. All rights reserved..

focus on helping victims of natural disasters instead of suicidal web surfers.

Losing our donors put our operation in jeopardy. Not only did I constantly worry about finances, I began to focus on all the hurting people we were reaching. Suddenly, I began to feel no matter how many resources I had, no matter how much I did, it wouldn't be enough. I began to feel sucked into the sea of depression along with the multitudes already there. I was the captain of a lifeboat with limited seating, sent out to rescue the masses. I felt the desperation of the drowning souls around me and like their desperation could pull our little lifeboat beneath the waves.

One morning, I turned on the radio and heard a Christian worship leader say, "Whatever you've focused on is what you worship."

I had a horrible thought. Could it be I was somehow worshipping the sea of depression? Surely not.

Worrying about the lost was my task, I reasoned, *the burden God had given me. My job was to grieve for those who were hurting and lost without God. Right?*

Perhaps, but wasn't my main focus was supposed to be the Lord?

Oh Lord, I prayed. *I'd much rather focus on you than on the hurting. Of course I know you've called me to help. But I know you care about the hurting even more than I do. But they're not to be my focus. You are.*

I was flooded with relief.

The sea of depression was no longer my burden; it was God's burden. I didn't have to obsess about the money to fund our program. That was God's problem. And true to form, he took care of it. My donors returned and all the bills were soon paid in full. We ended the year with money to spare.

I explained this to one of my ministry partners who said, "Did you know that the ministers of the past who focused on the hurting, in a fanatical sort of way, *became* the hurting? They all dealt with terrible pain in their bodies.

Yikes!

Recently my single friend said, "After becoming a widow, over a decade ago, my whole prayer life has been focused on finding the right man to date. Could it be the hope of dating the perfect man is what I worship?"

She was horrified at the revelation and we agreed it was time to turn her focus back to the Lord. After all, God could worry about finding the "perfect man" for her—in his time and according to his plan. He could cause the relationship she'd dreamed of to come into being, or not. The point is, God knows the desires of my friend's heart. When she gives God her whole heart, she'll find the happiness she longs for, with or without "the perfect man."

Be careful that your prayer concerns don't become your focus above God. We focus on God because he demands it and as we discussed, one of God's names is Jealous. We read in Exodus, 34:14, "Do not worship any other god, for the LORD, whose name is Jealous, is a jealous God."

Again, God is not jealous *of* us. He's jealous *for* us.

As humans, our number one job, our reason for existence, is to worship God. God demands worship, not because he is prideful, but because walking with him is in our best interest. Walking with God is what we were made for. It's how we find both purpose and fulfillment. Have you ever wondered why it's okay for God to be jealous, but it's not okay for us humans? Well, for us humans, jealously is spelled p-r-i-d-e and pride is the opposite of worship. When we are prideful, we don't worship God, we worship ourselves. Proverbs 8:13 (TLB) put it this way, "If anyone respects and fears God, he will hate evil. For wisdom hates pride, arrogance, corruption, and deceit of every kind."

Has God created rules to show us how to avoid pride, arrogance, corruption, and deceit? Yep. He even used his finger to carve in stone a list of rules for us to follow. You may have seen the 1923 Cecil B. DeMille version of *The Ten Commandments*, but wait until you see how it's told in *The God You Need To Know*, a version which actually predates Hollywood itself.

Talk about epic productions. It took heaven and earth (under God's direction with special effects including seven deadly plagues) to move the Egyptian Pharaoh to free his slaves so they could follow Moses to the Promised Land.

Can you imagine Moses leading three million men, women and children into and through the Red Sea and into the desert? After a three months journey, Moses led the people to Mount Sinai, the Holy Mountain of God where God's voice thundered in smoke, mist and lightening. Let's roll the tape as God's people quaked at the sound of God's voice. Finally, they had enough. "Moses! Speak to us yourself and we will listen. But do not have God speak to us or we will die."

Moses replied, "Do not be afraid. God has come to test you, so that the fear of God will be with you to keep you from sinning" (Ex 20:18-20).

In this next scene, Moses climbs the mountain where God carves his Ten Commandments into stone tablets. For forty days Moses tarries with God, then returns to his people. As he approaches the camp, he stops to listen to the sound of singing but when he sees his people bow to the golden calf they've made from their own earrings, he explodes in a rage, smashing the stone tablets.

Moses is not the only one who's angry. God himself is angry enough to wipe out the entire nation. In fact, 3000 Israelites died that day. But Moses pleas for the lives of his people and God's anger passes. Then once again, God carves his ten rules upon new stone tablets.

What's so important about these Ten Commandments that God would write them in stone—twice? For starters, these words of God were meant to help us walk with him.

Dr. Barry McCarty of the Christian's Hour radio program says, "Even though Christians are, as the book of Romans says, not under the law but under the gospel, the Ten Commandments are still a good path for living. They are still a picture into the heart and character of God. They are still those basic bedrock principles, which God expects us to build our lives; the compass to give us our moral bearings."[30]

Without God's rules to set our moral compass to truth, we would spin out of control, hopelessly lost. There's danger ignoring any one of the Ten Commandments because skipping one rule could result in a shipwrecked life.

Let's take a close look at each of God's ten rules found in the twentieth chapter of Exodus. If these are God's rules to live by, they must be sweet and easy to follow, right? Let's take a look at the first commandment, *"I am the LORD your God, who brought you out of Egypt, out of the land of slavery. You shall have no other gods before me"* (1-3).

This is an easy one, that is, if you can ensure your major focus is on God in all areas of your life.

---

[30] Dr. Barry McCarty quote from *The Christian's Hour Broadcast*, Thursday July 27, 2006, www.oneplace.com, © Copyright 2006, Oneplace.com. All rights reserved.

Hmmm, that sounds kinda difficult, actually.

Well, maybe the next rule is easier... *"You shall not make for yourself an idol in the form of anything in heaven above or on the earth beneath or in the waters below. You shall not bow down to them or worship them; for I, the LORD your God, am a jealous God, punishing the children for the sin of the fathers to the third and fourth generation of those who hate me, but showing love to a thousand [generations] of those who love me and keep my commandments"* (4-6).

Whew! We don't have graven images in our lives, do we? Theologian John Calvin thinks we do. He said, "Human sin, inherited from Adam and Eve, produces in each person an 'idol factory.'" [31]

He could be right, especially considering what C. S. Lewis wrote his fictional book, *The Screwtape Letters* about this topic. He portrays a senior demon writing letters of instruction to his diabolical nephew, Wormwood. The letters are meant to teach Wormword the finer points of tempting his 'human assignment' away from God. Evil Screwtape writes, "I have known cases where what the patient called his 'God' was actually located —up and to the left of the corner of the bedroom ceiling, or inside his own head, or in a crucifix on the wall. But whatever the nature of the composite object, you must keep him praying to it—to the thing that he has made, not to the Person who has made him."[32]

Is that what we really look like when *we're* praying? *I hope not.*

---

[31] John Calvin quote, http://www.island-of-freedom.com/CALVIN.HTM.
[32] C. S. Lewis, *The Screwtape Letters* (San Francisco, CA, Harper San Francisco © 1942, C.S. Lewis Pte. Ltd. Copyright restored © 1966 C.S. Lewis Pte. Ltd,), P. 18.

Well, this next rule has got to be easier… *"You shall not misuse the name of the LORD your God, for the LORD will not hold anyone guiltless who misuses his name"* (7).

My brother often hands out pennies with the Ten Commandments stamped on them at the Mississippi State Fair. The Ten Commandments usually lead him into some interesting discussions. Jimmy often asks, "Have you ever taken God's name in vain?"

Yes, most people will admit to that.

Jimmy then asks, "Did you know that the word says God will not count you guiltless? He reports most people respond by giving him a kind of a deer-caught-in-the-headlights look.

Oh dear!

Okay, let's move on. Is it just me, or were the first few commandments difficult to perfectly maintain? Surely the next one will be easier to accomplish. *"Remember the Sabbath day by keeping it holy. Six days you shall labor and do all your work, but the seventh day is a Sabbath to the LORD your God. On it you shall not do any work, neither you, nor your son or daughter, nor your manservant or maidservant, nor your animals, nor the alien within your gates. For in six days the LORD made the heavens and the earth, the sea, and all that is in them, but he rested on the seventh day. Therefore the LORD blessed the Sabbath day and made it holy"* (8-11).

In other words, the Lord rested on the Sabbath and he's asking you to rest so that you can spend time with him. Do you always hold up your end of the bargain? I wish I could claim I've lived this out perfectly, but I've fallen short here too.

I'm certain there's got to be at least one we can all get right. How about, *"Honor your father and your mother, so that you may live long in the land the LORD your God is giving you"* (12).

In our last chapter, we learned this was the commandment the Pharisees cheated on. If they dedicated or set aside their money to the church, they didn't feel obligated to help their parents financially.

Today this commandment is often broken in a more horrendous way. Imagine the doctor explains, "Your Mom is dying, or will certainly die someday, so the merciful thing to do is to dehydrate her to death. This will avoid expensive therapies as well as any hope for recovery."

I may have exaggerated a bit as this may not be the exact wording a doctor would use. However he might say, "Let's do the merciful thing. Your mom wouldn't want to live without quality of life, would she?"

Really? My daughter loves her quality of life as a handicapped person.

Watch out, this quick way to get your inheritance may violate God's taboo when it comes to "Honoring your father and mother." Of course, there is a time appointed to die, but that's for God to decide. A life cut short outside of God's laws may miss out on closure with family and even with God. So don't be fooled by euthanasia rhetoric. It even violates the next commandment, *"You shall not murder"* (13).

What more can I say?

The next commandment is, *"You shall not commit adultery"* (14). If you're older than five minutes, you know that commandment is often broken. Several years ago, Pastor Adrian Rogers said, "Cohabitation was illegal in the United States until about 1970. Since then, it has increased 600 percent...that's tragic. Sometimes we have couples come to join our church. We notice they have the same address but they don't have the same last name. We tell them to get right with God, they are going to have to get married.

"...God's word forbids people living together without the benefit of marriage. When God says, "Though shalt," he's saying help yourself to happiness. When he says, "Though shalt not," he's saying, "Don't hurt yourself.'"[33]

Please know it's not for me to judge anyone. Judgment belongs to God and God alone. These commandments seem to have a way of stepping on our toes.

The next commandment is, *"You shall not steal"* (15). Now, this is a commandment my brother tells me almost everyone will admit to breaking when he gives his Ten Commandments checkup. He'll ask, "Have you ever stolen a pencil?

"Yes."

"Well, that makes you a thief."

OUCH!

Next my bother discusses the "no lying" commandment; *"You shall not give false testimony against your neighbor"* (16).

He asks, "Have you ever told a lie?"

Usually he wins yet another confession and Jimmy says, "I guess that makes you a liar."

You'd think by this point, Jimmy's conversations would abruptly end. But he says, "People want the truth. I've presented these questions over a thousand times and only one person was ever offended."

Interesting.

And now, we need a drum roll because we've found ourselves at the tenth and final commandment—which I sometimes find to be a difficult one; *"You shall not covet your neighbor's house. You shall not covet your neighbor's wife, or his manservant or maidservant, his ox or donkey, or anything that belongs to your neighbor"* (17).

Envy is actually a form of pride. How I hate to aim it at someone else or to feel its aim at me. Once a dear friend admitted she was jealous of my ministry. I told her, "We bloom in season to serve a divine purpose. That's why we can't compare ourselves to one another. For God has planted us both and he will make sure both of our purposes bloom for the good in the right season. We are on the same team. We are not in competition."

Back to the Mississippi State Fair. My brother follows up on his Ten Commandment discussions with, "You told me at the beginning of our conversation you were a pretty good person, especially when you compare yourselves with others. But you've just compared yourself with God's standard and as you can see, you don't measure up. It's kind of like looking at a flock of sheep on the hillside and marveling at the whiteness of their wool. Until it snows. When the sheep are surrounded by pure white snow, you'll see how dirty the sheep really are. You see the dirt when you compare to a higher standard."

He continues, "James 2:10-11 says, 'For whoever keeps the whole law and yet stumbles at just one point is guilty of breaking all of it. For he who said, 'Do not commit adultery,' also said, 'Do not murder.' If you do not commit adultery but do commit murder, you have become a lawbreaker.'"

"If this is so, then that means we are all (me and you included) are lawbreakers. We're in a lot of trouble with God."

Jimmy adds, "Yet, despite the fact that none of us meet God's standard, we have hope. Romans 3:21-24 says, 'But now a righteousness from God, apart from law, has been made known, to which the Law and the Prophets testify. This righteousness from God comes through faith in Jesus Christ to all who believe. There is no difference, for all have sinned and fall short of the glory of God, and are justified freely by his grace through the redemption that came by Christ Jesus.'"

Jimmy asks, "Have you heard of the guy who missed heaven by eighteen inches? He knew who God was – in his head, not in his heart.

"It's kind of like the President. You may know who he is, but that doesn't mean you know him personally."[34]

The bottom line is God, through Jesus and his work on the cross, has the power to forgive us for breaking his laws. (thank goodness!)

We certainly need to be reconciled with God. Here are some tips that help in growing our relationship with him:

- When we focus on his holiness, we see our sins.
- When we focus on his son Jesus, we see that he became our sin on the cross.
- When we ask God, through Jesus to forgive our sins, he does so.
- Thank you Lord!

This simple message may need to be replayed a few times before we move it the eighteen inches from our heads to our hearts. If you've been considering a relationship with

---

[34] Jimmy Evans' Ten Commandment penny presentation adapted from Ray Comfort's *Hell's Best Kept Secrets* (New Kensington, PA, Whitaker House; Expanded edition, 2004).

God, now might be a good time to turn the above points into your own prayer.

Walking With God Through Obedience

If you love God, you will serve him. You will honor him by following his Ten Commandments as closely as you can. Not because that's where you find your hope, it's because that's how you show God your love.

Also consider, if you knew God was calling you to step out in faith to accomplish some great work for him, would you take the next step, or like Jonah, would you run the other way? I think we really never know until we're tested…

…One morning, as I was waking up, I asked God to guide my steps as well as my words. I'd been attending the Christian Booksellers Tradeshow. Getting ready to walk down to the Denver Convention Center for an appointment, I felt led to wear my press badge for my electronic magazine, *Right to the Heart of Women*, instead of my author's badge—even though I'd planned meetings with book publishers.

However, my walk to the convention center was divinely delayed. I soon discovered that Michael Schiavo was about to host a press conference in my hotel in a nearby conference room. Schiavo, as you might recall, was the Florida man who convinced the courts to euthanize his disabled wife, Terri Schiavo, in 2005.

When I found myself standing at the open door of the conference room where Michael's press conference was about to be begin, I was absolutely stunned. Though I'd prayed for a chance to tell Michael what I thought about the public execution of his disabled wife, now I wasn't sure if that's what God wanted me to do. Then I remembered my early morning prayer, *"God, guide my steps and my words."*

I quietly inquired to the Lord for instruction and he answered in the secret depths of my heart, "What do you think? You're camera ready and wearing a press badge."

"Okay, Lord, I'm going in, but *please* go in with me."

A few minutes later, with me sitting on the front row, the press conference started. Michael was there to garner sympathy and support for his cause of euthanasia and the right he believed every American should have to dehydrate an ill or disabled family member. After the intense legal battle he'd won against Terri's mother and family, over *his* right to kill his wife, he'd come to complain. He said, "The government interfered with my will, my wishes, and my family." But his next two words surprised me. "Questions anyone?"

I raised a trembling hand and said, "I'm the mother of a disabled adult. What about Terri's parents, I understand the legalities, but weren't her parents her family too?"

Michael leapt from his chair. He let his red-faced fury loose in front of the Denver media as he screamed, "They lost their rights to her when she married me. *Do you get that?*"

Yes, I got it. And I was happy to grant an interview with Denver's *9News* to express my thoughts on the matter a few minutes later.[35]

I didn't tell you this story to make a political statement. I told it to ask you a question. What will you do when God places you at your door of opportunity? When your knees are knocking, will you be obedient? Will you pray, "Lord, I'm going in, please go in with me?" *Please do*. Please go where God calls you. Not before him, but through him. For

---

[35] Schiavo story adapted from *Right to the Heart of Women Ezine*, © 2006 from www.RightToTheHeartOfWomen.com.

when you worship God through obedience, you not only walk with him, he walks with and in you.

Love Notes:

In this chapter we see:

- Whatever we focus on more than God is what we worship.

- Outside of God, we become enslaved to that which we worship.

- We were created to worship God, worshiping anyone or anything else but God is dangerous.

- God's Ten Commandments are meant to protect us from harm.

- We obey God because we love him and because we want to walk with him.

Worship Experience:

We all worship something and each thing we worship demands a sacrifice.

Experience One:

Read the following Psalm aloud:

> *Our God is in heaven;*
> *he does whatever pleases him.*
> *But their idols are silver and gold,*
> *made by the hands of men.*
> *They have mouths, but cannot speak,*
> *eyes, but they cannot see;*
> *they have ears, but cannot hear,*
> *noses, but they cannot smell;*
> *they have hands, but cannot feel,*
> *feet, but they cannot walk;*
> *nor can they utter a sound with their throats.*
> *Those who make them will be like them,*

and so will all who trust in them.
(Ps 115:3-8)

Experience Two:

It's time to put your idols away. List every major focus of your life here; include your joys, worries and stresses:

_____

_____

_____

Experience Three:

Next, plug your list, one at a time, into the following prayer:

Dear Lord,

I tear down my altar to: _____. I give you: _____. I give you my worries and concerns regarding: _____.

Please worry about this for me. I focus on you. I thank you for how you will help me concerning: _____ and praise you for what you are going to do.

I look to you.

In Jesus' name,

Amen

Experience Four

Next, after you've prayed through your entire list, let's take out the trash. First read: Ps. 51:4, "Against you, you only, have I sinned and done what is evil in your sight."

Now pray:

Dear Lord,

I'm thinking though my sins, and putting them, one by one, into the trash.

I hand you the trashcan. I know this is a stinky gift but I want my heart and soul to be pure before you.

Please forgive me for these sins and help me to turn away from them.

In Jesus' Name

Amen.

Chapter 5

Divine Design

We came from the womb equipped for connectivity with God, pre-wired to praise. – Louie Giglio[36]

God has a divine design. We can discover this design by studying the secrets held in the Ark of the Covenant. But first a little background...

Did you see the movie *Raiders of the Lost Ark,*[37] starring Harrison Ford? Let me give you a quick synopsis of the storyline. The year is 1936. Archeology professor Indiana Jones has been hired by the government of the United Stated to find THE lost Ark of the Covenant believed to hold the Ten Commandments. Unfortunately, the agents of Hitler are also after the Ark. Why? They believe the famed Ark will give them God's power if they can but possess it. But will Indiana Jones find the Ark before it falls into the wrong hands?

Perhaps the real question is this; can we find the missing Ark of the Covenant?

It's really missing.

To kick off our investigation as to its whereabouts I'll play the theme music of the *Raiders* movie while I rewind *The God You Need To Know* to the scene where the Hebrews are escaping Pharaoh's army.

Just Follow the Cloud

Quiet on the set!

---

[36] Louie Giglio, *The Air I Breathe*, Inc. P. 14.
[37] *Raiders of the Lost Ark*, directed by Stephen Spielberg and starring Harrison Ford, Karen Allen, Paul Freeman, produced by Lucasfilm and Paramont, 1981.

Well, that's impossible with three million men, women and children, and former slaves of Egypt milling about. What a commotion they make as they try to escape the Pharaoh's army.

Fortunately, the Hebrews have a secret weapon, a weapon that covers them until every last one crossed the path of dry land that split the Red Sea, a path God-created only moments earlier. Is the secret weapon the path itself? No, it's something more. Listen to the narrator describe it as the camera follows the Hebrew people as they journey beyond captivity.

> **Narrator:** By day the LORD went ahead of them in a pillar of cloud to guide them on their way and by night in a pillar of fire to give them light, so that they could travel by day or night. Neither the pillar of cloud by day nor the pillar of fire by night left its place in front of the people (Ex 13:21-22).

This is incredible. God's glory (in the form of a cloud) led his people to Mount Sinai, the place where God would soon present the Ten Commandments to Moses.

Later, when the Israelites made camp at the base of the holy mountain, Moses climbed into the glory cloud that cloaked the mountainside. In fact, when Moses brought the Ten Commandments back to camp the second time, after spending another forty days with God, he glowed so brightly the Hebrews made him wear a veil.

The cloud then, is a major clue. But my question is this — where did the cloud go after it left the mountain?

The Tabernacle of God

While camped at Mount Sinai, God instructed Moses and his people to make a tabernacle, a portable tent of worship, to specifications so exact it takes seven chapters — a total of 243 verses to describe its design. Why did God specify so many details? I believe the detail is meant to denote the tabernacle's significance. It was to be a place to house the glory of God.

The people created this tent of worship out of the treasures given to them by their former captors; gold, silver and bronze; fabrics of fine linen, purple, and scarlet; exotic animal skins; acacia wood; lamp oil; spices and incense; onyx and other gem stones.

How rich. But we can see that for ourselves as the camera pans round the entire tent structure. First there's the outer court where the people worshipped God. This outer court, 150 by 75 feet, has four walls fashioned out of linen drapes fastened to brass posts. Also inside this court is where the priests sacrificed animals to God on altars. Just past the altars stands the tent of the Tabernacle itself a place so sacred only the priests could enter.

Let's reverently take a look at the inside of the Tabernacle's two special rooms. The first room is called the Holy Place with its golden candlesticks (representing the light of God's word and will), incense (a special blend used only by God believed to cover the stench of the sin) and tables full of fresh bread (representing God's provision). Past the final curtain of scarlet and purple is the most sacred room in the Tabernacle — the Holy of Holies.

Listen! The Tabernacle choir is singing and their voices swell with harmony and power, "H-a-l-l-e-l-u-j-a-h."

Hush and be reverent, we've found the clue we're looking for; *the cloud is here.* God's presence is in the Holy of Holies, a place so sacred only the High Priest could enter once a year on the Day of Atonement. We shouldn't go inside, but if we could we'd see the object we came to find nestled behind the curtain, the Ark of the Covenant.

The Ark of the Covenant

What makes this Ark so special? Let's discuss its specifications — the Ark is a box made of wood covered with gold. It is about four feet long two and a half feet wide, two and a half feet high, and filled with secrets.

But wait. As sacred as the Ark of the Covenant is, we need to understand that it was not the actual object of worship. The people worshipped the presence of God that rested on the Ark's lid, the Mercy Seat.

Are you ready see what's inside the Ark of the Covenant? There are three sacred items:

- **A jar containing Manna from heaven** — This actual sample represents God's provision. Every morning, in the days of the Exodus, God would cover the ground with fresh Manna (a bread-like substance,) the people would gather and eat.

- **The Ten Commandants** — This represents God's law.

- **The staff of Aaron** — Used to resolve a dispute in the camp. It seems God showed favor on Aaron, Moses' brother, by causing his staff to not only blossom but to produce almonds. This once dead stick represents resurrection.

But here's the topper, as I mentioned, the Ark of the Covenant has a golden lid called the Mercy Seat. On either end of this lid are golden cherubim, winged creatures that look both animal and human. They represent both heaven's and creation's continual worship of God. Notice how their wings stretch as if to shield the Mercy Seat.

The Mercy Seat is the very place where the presence of God rested. It's the place the High Priest sprinkled the blood of a bullock to cover the sins of the people and it's also where God meets us with his covenant. More than an object or place, it's God's act of forgiveness.

Walking with God

The Ark has a colorful history. It never stayed in one place for long, especially as it traveled with the Hebrews on their trek though the desert.

Watch this clip as God's glory moves out of the tabernacle before hovering in front of the camp to indicate it's time to move. Watch the priests break down the temple into portable pieces, ready to follow God's glory deeper into the wilderness.

Did you notice how the priests carried the Ark? Forbidden to touch it, they used golden poles inserted into special loops to carry the Ark whenever God's presence led them. This ensured the priests and the people always walked in the presence of God. However, because the people had so much trouble following God, it took them forty years to get across the desert to the place God had promised them.

But one glorious day, the priests carried the Ark of the Covenant across the Jordan River and into the Promised Land. When the men and women gathered at the River Jordan, God rolled back the river and the people once again passed through the waters and onto dry land. God continued to make a way so they could cross into the land of promise *with* the presence of God.

But what happened to the Ark of the Covenant after it finally arrived in the promised land? The Ark continued to entertain adventure. For example, at the Battle of Jericho, the people marched and blew their trumpets as the priests carried the Ark around the walls of the city. After seven trips, the presence and power of God caused Jericho's walls to tumble and the city was defeated. (Joshua 6)

As long as God's presence went before the people, the people were safe, victorious and prosperous. That's a valuable clue to help us find the Ark's current location. But to understand this clue to its fullest, we have to answer the question; what happened when the people went *ahead* of God's presence?

Listen! The Raider of the Lost Ark theme music has cranked up, setting the mood for this next bit of real-life Ark adventure...

Ashdod was a Philistine city on the Mediterranean Sea and its people worshiped Dagon, a god who was part fish. The Israelites decided to carry the Ark of the Covenant into battle against the Philistines because they thought its presence would keep them from being defeated.

Wrong!

They'd failed to seek God with this plan, mainly because they felt it was their right to use God as they wanted. How shocked they were when they were defeated in battle and the Philistines captured the Ark.

But good news, it didn't take long before the Philistines returned the Ark. How could they not after what happened when they placed the Ark in Dagon's temple. The very first night the idol of Dagon toppled face down before the Ark. The Philistines righted their god, but the very next day, the idol was not only toppled, it's head and hands were lopped off.

OOPS!

After that a series of terrible plagues and diseases swept through the city of Ashdod and the Philistines sent the Ark back to Israel. (Who can blame them?)

The presence of God is not a toy to be tinkered with. That was sort of the point of the movie Raiders of the Lost

Ark. In this fictional drama about the most holy of relics, the Nazis manage to acquire the Ark. But even when it was in their possession they didn't possess it.

And that's a lesson for us all. We can't own or manage God. Not only is it not our place, it's impossible.

Now, back to our mystery, *what finally became of the Ark?*

According to the *The Family Bible Encyclopedia Volume One*, "David finally brought the ark to Jerusalem. After Solomon built the Temple, there was a great ceremony as the ark was placed in the Temple (1 Kings 8:1-21).

"When Jerusalem and the Temple were destroyed by the Babylonians in 586 B.C., the ark was lost forever. There was no ark in the second Temple nor in the Temple built by Herod the Great shortly before the time of Christ."[38]

If the ark is still missing how do we find it? Remember our first clue? *Follow the cloud.*

Where does the cloud appear next? The Raiders of the Lost Ark music is blaring through the stereo as I fast forward *The God You Need To Know* past the time of the judges, past the time of the kings and prophets, past a stable in Bethlehem...past...oh, we're there. Watch the screen for the next appearance of the cloud...

The Cloud Reappears

It's a sunny day as Jesus and his disciples, Peter, James and his brother John take a walk up a steep mountain trail.

When they reach the top, Jesus begins to glow--his face shining like the sun and his clothes white as light. Moses and the famous prophet Elijah suddenly appear in the brightness surrounding them.

---

[38] Berkeley & Alvera Mickelsen, *The Family Bible Encyclopedia Volume One*, (Colorado Springs, CO: David C. Cook Publishing Company, 1978) P. 31.

Peter can't contain himself. "Lord, it is good for us to be here. If you wish, I will put up three shelters-one for you, one for Moses and one for Elijah."

While Peter's still speaking, a bright cloud envelops them and God's voice surrounds them, "This is my Son, whom I love; with him I am well pleased. Listen to him" (Matt 17:1-5)!

Look—Jesus is in the cloud! Could Jesus himself have the secret instructions to help us find the lost Ark?

This is a good clue because we see Jesus in the cloud one more time. But this time it's forty days after his death and resurrection. It's the day he was *taken away* by the cloud in the middle of a conversation with his followers.

Suddenly two men dressed in white stood beside those left behind. "Men of Galilee," they said, "why do you stand here looking into the sky? This same Jesus, who has been taken from you into heaven, will come back in the same way you have seen him go into heaven" (Acts 1:9-11).

Oh wow. Now my question is with Jesus leaving inside the cloud, has God's removed his presence from us? Are we now alone, waiting for Jesus to someday reappear in the clouds (Luke 21:27)? Will we never find the Ark of the Covenant?

Consider this – we are now under a new covenant of God's design. That means THE ARK IS NOT LOST! IT IS WITHIN US!

It's true, when we trust in Jesus, deciding to follow after him, we start to carry the very presence of God's Holy Spirit within ourselves. Our very bodies have become the new temple. The sacred box or the Ark itself is our own hearts. God still meets us at the Mercy Seat, as our hearts are sprinkled with the blood of Jesus.

And Jesus is in our hearts. He's the:

- **Manna from heaven** — the provision; the bread of life.

- **The Ten Commandants** — the fulfillment of God's law.

- **The staff of Aaron** — the resurrection.

Did you have any idea the Ark was so near? God's master plan to defeat Satan and to rescue us from the dominion of darkness worked flawlessly. We are no longer kidnapped, for we walk with God and his spirit lives inside of us. The poles that carry the Ark are now our very own legs as our bodies are his temple.

No longer does the Holy of Holies have a thick veil to separate God from man. At the moment of Jesus' death on the cross, the double veil that hung in the Jerusalem temple split by an unseen hand from the top to the bottom. The split veil signifies God is no longer hidden from man.

How does finding the lost Ark of the Covenant help us take our places with God? We have broken free from our captor and can now walk with God.

Paul wrote in a letter to the church of Ephesians,

"For this reason I kneel before the Father, from whom his whole family in heaven and on earth derives its name. I pray that out of his glorious riches he may strengthen you with power through his Spirit in your inner being, so that Christ may dwell in your hearts through faith. And I pray that you, being rooted and established in love, may have power, together with all the saints, to grasp how wide and long and high and deep is the love of Christ, and to know this love that surpasses knowledge-that you may be filled to the measure of all the fullness of God.

"Now to him who is able to do immeasurably more than all we ask or imagine, according to his power that is at work within us, to him be glory in the church and in Christ Jesus throughout all generations, for ever and ever! Amen" (Eph 3:14-21).

Rejoice! We are under a new Ark of the Covenant – one sealed with the blood of Christ. What does the new Ark of the Covenant means to us? It means we can:

1. Entertain God's very presence.
2. Enjoy forgiveness of sin.
3. Follow God's guidance.
4. Enjoy God's provision.
5. Enjoy God's grace and mercy.
6. Rejoice in Christ's resurrection.
7. Worship.

Love Notes:

Our own bodies can now contain the presence of God's glory! There's only one thing to do with this news; REJOICE!

Worship Experiences:

Experience One:

We'll go on a worship experience to tear down the altars in our lives that aren't dedicated to the LORD.

Read Deut 12:2-4, "Destroy completely all the places on the high mountains and on the hills and under every spreading tree where the nations you are dispossessing worship their gods. Break down their altars, smash their sacred stones and burn their Asherah poles in the fire; cut down the idols of their gods and wipe out their names from those places.

"You must not worship the LORD your God in their way."

I know this is similar to what we did in the last chapter, but it's so important, we need to continue to contemplate the struggle. Make a list of things you may have a secret altar to in your heart:

Below I will make a list of suggestions to help you determine if you pay homage to anything besides God. Note: By homage I mean, ask yourself, have I put this item or desire veer my thoughts and worship of God? Check all that may apply:

___Secret Altars	___Spending
___Sexual appetites	___My Time
___Money	___Any kind of sin
___Prestige	___Food
___Fame	___Home
___Entertainments	___Car
___Job	___Collecting/Collections
___Family	___Contests
___Hobbies	___Sports
___Games	___Movies
___Pornography	___Shopping
___Television	___Envy
___Hero Worship	___School
___The News or Media	___Dating
___Troubles	___Not Dating
___Pain	___Marriage/Spouse

___Fear   ___Politics

___Worry   ___Debt

___Regret   ___Others_____

Check off anything that you may think about MORE or may be MORE important to you than God. Another question to ask yourself is, do you ignore any of God's laws or direction to spend time with, thinking about, or doing any of these things? If so, you have an altar to a false god.

Remember, if you're somehow spending time worshipping any of these desires, interests or pastimes, you will become its slave. It's time you get set free. It's time to tear all altars that aren't to God.

Please note, I'm not asking you to tear down your marriage or your family, or other good things God has given you. I'm simply asking you to be careful not to put anything, even good things, before God.

There are two kinds of false gods. 1. The gods of sin and frets; 2. The gods of life's good things. If your altar is to one of the gods of sins and frets, here's what to pray.

Dear Lord, I give you my worship of (worry.)

I lay that down at your feet.

Please forgive me for putting my worship of (worry) before you. Help me to put you first and to establish the boundaries you would have me create. I tear down my altar to (worry) and worship you.

In Jesus' name,

Amen.

When the altar is to one of life's good things, here's what to pray to put it back in its proper place.

Dear Lord, I give you my worship of (family.)

I lay my worship of (family) down at your feet.

Please forgive me for putting my worship of (family) before you. Help me to put you first and to love (family) for and through you. Give me the strength to love you more. I tear down my altar to (family) and worship you.

In Jesus' name,

Amen.

In the above prayer, you are not saying you no longer love your (family) you are saying you put God first and you will love your (family) through and for God.

This is called **balance**.

You may need to pray these prayers for everything on this list, and then some. Take the time to go through this exercise to clearly demonstrate that God, and only God, is who you worship.

Experience Two:

Write your own prayer or praise to God.

Chapter 6

Divine Victory

"For the battle is not yours, but God's." - 2 Chron 20:15b

An eight-year-old girl named Tiffany asked her ten-year-old brother, Sam, "What's bigger than God?"

Sam asked, "Can you give me a hint?"

"Well," Tiff grinned, "Poor people have it, rich people need it, believers lack it and atheists believe it. Can you guess what it is?"

Her brother scratched his head. "I can think of *nothing*."

Tiff looked disappointed. "Aw, you guessed it."

Tiff and Sam are right. Poor people have nothing, rich people need nothing, believers lack nothing, and atheists believe nothing. But most importantly of all, *nothing* is bigger than God, and that includes our problems as well as our battles.

Ask Elisha, one of God's prophets who lived during the reign of Israel's King Jehoram. Elisha was absolutely fearless, why? He knew God so well he knew he had nothing to fear, except God. I'll forward *The God You Need To Know* so you can see for yourself...

...This clip starts with Elisha rushing to confer with Jehoram, the King of Israel. God had been whispering into Elisha's ear, telling him the King of Syria's secret plans to attack Israel. Because Elisha tells Jehoram Syria's plans, Jehoram is able to sidestep the Syrian ambush.

Meanwhile back in Syria, the Syrian King has a royal tantrum upon learning his ambush failed. He wails, "Who has been repeating the words I speak in my own bedroom to the King of Israel?"

His servant trembles and then stutters, "No one but that prophet, Elisha, your majesty."

"BRING HIM TO ME!"

Uh Oh!! Elisha's in trouble now.

A few days later, it's a beautiful morning in the city of Dothan. But Elisha's servant almost drops his water jar when he sees Syrian soldiers, horses and chariots surrounding the city. The leader of the soldiers calls out to this lad. "Bring us Elisha!"

The boy scampers back to Elisha's abode. "Master, what shall we do?"

Watch how Elisha responds…

…He shrugs. "Fear not. Those that are with us are more than are with them." He calls out in prayer, "Lord, open my servant's eyes so he may see."

Look at the angelic host of warring angels in their chariots of fire as they fill the skies. Trouble is, only Elisha and his servant can see them.

Elisha calls to the Lord, "Lord, strike down this Syrian army with blindness."

Look! The soldiers fall into confusion as they lose their sight. But Elisha hurries to help them. "Soldiers of Syria, you're in the wrong place. The man you seek is in another city. Here, let me show you the way."

Here's the funny part; watch as Elisha leads this blind army into the heart of the city of Samaria, a stronghold of the Israelites. He prays for the sight of the soldiers to return. When it does, they're surrounded by the Israelite army!

OOPS!

Now King Jehoram could have lopped off the heads of these enemy soldiers, but Elisha intervenes. "King, feed them and send them home."

King Jehoram obliges and the Syrian army is sent home with its tail between its legs. When the King of Syria hears how well his men were treated while in captivity, his heart is moved and he quits trying to make war with Israel. (Paraphrased 2 Kings 6:1 -23.) Amazing. The battle was won without bloodshed on either side. That's the kind of victory that can only come from God.

Why wasn't Elisha afraid?

- He knew God.

- He heard God.

- He saw God's provision.

In fact, it was Elisha's knowledge of God that somehow shrunk and weakened his enemy. But unlike the family in the movie, *Honey, I Shrunk the Kids*, Elisha's enemy had no idea they were small and powerless.

Did you know that God sees our enemies as:

1. Lacking truth.

2. Blind.

3. Surrounded.

4. In captivity.

5. Able to change when love is applied?

Just understanding these secrets will also give you the advantage as you begin to understand those who are with you are more in number than those who are with your enemy. Let's thank God:

Thank you Lord,

Thank you that you are greater and more powerful than my problems or my enemies. Open my eyes and let me see that greater are those who are with me than those who are my problems and enemies. I give and lead my problems and enemies to you. Show my problems and enemies you have surrounded them and they are defeated. I trust these situations to you - for you are my Lord and my protector.

In Jesus' name,

Amen.

What a powerful prayer. Next, you need to encounter God in order to obtain and carry out your marching orders.

Encounter God Before You Encounter Your Enemy

Imagine this, you are minding your own business, threshing your grain in the wine press. Huh? What's wrong with this picture?

Let me introduce you to Gideon who was hiding from his enemies, the Midianites, by sifting his grain in an unlikely place, a wine press. It's his hope that his secret location will keep the roving bands of hoodlums from swooping in to steal his crop.

But when Gideon walks out of his hideout and into the sunshine, he has an interesting encounter. He finds an angel of the Lord sitting beneath an oak tree.

Watch as the angel says, "The Lord is with you, you mighty man of valor."

Gideon replies, "The Lord? He's abandoned us. He made promises he didn't keep. (Judges 6:11-13 paraphrased.)

I'll freeze this frame. After a bit of banter, Gideon, to his great embarrassment, realizes he's talking to an angel who came to deliver a message. God has called Gideon to destroy the enemy of his people. But before the angel of the Lord reveals more, he gives Gideon a little assignment. Gideon is to tear down the altar to Baal located on a hill on his dad's property and replace it with an altar to God. Next, Gideon is to sacrifice his father's seven-year-old bull. (Are you kidding? This would be on par with a modern kid crashing his father's Porsche into the house.)

Gideon's afraid to obey, so afraid, he waits till dark. The next morning, his father and the townspeople are shocked to find an altar to Jehovah has replaced their altar to their favorite god. These neighbors set out to kill Gideon. But Gideon's father faces the angry mob on Gideon's behalf. "Are you going to plead Baal's cause? Are you trying to save him? Whoever fights for him shall be put to death by morning! If Baal really is a god, he can defend himself when someone breaks down his altar" (Judges 6:31).

Let's review this scene. So far, God has:

1. Called Gideon.
2. Called Gideon to a purpose.
3. Called Gideon to obedience.

Notice, before God uses Gideon, he tests Gideon. But after Gideon passes the test, Gideon tests God. When I say 'tests God,' I don't mean Gideon tests God to see how great God is. He tests God to see if he has the correct marching orders. In other words, he's trying to ask God, *"You say you want me to do **what**?"*

While Gideon and his dad were busy facing the angry mob, their nation's enemies were moving into position to attack them. When Gideon hears the news, he's led by the spirit of God to call his nation to war. Suddenly thirty-two thousand men stream in from every corner of his land, ready to follow him into battle.

But Gideon is uncertain. Does God really want him, a farmer, to lead an attack against their enemy? Forget the angel, forget the enemy is ready to attack, and forget the sudden appearance of thirty-two thousand men ready to follow him into battle, Gideon wants another sign. Watch him as he prays and asks God to take a sheepskin and to soak it with dew while he sleeps.

The next morning, we see Gideon wring a bowl of water out of the fleece. But Gideon isn't convinced. He conducts another test reversing his original prayer. "Do not be angry with me. Let me make just one more request. Allow me one more test with the fleece. This time make the fleece dry and the ground covered with dew."

The next morning, once again, God answers Gideon's request with a dry fleece on a wet ground. Gideon's now certain of his call and he obediently accepts his marching orders.

(Personally, I don't blame Gideon for checking in with God. How many times do we assume we know the mind of God, then plow ahead with our own plans?)

To follow Gideon's example, before we march into battle we should:

1. Meet God.

2. Obey God.

3. Inquire of God for direction.

Relying on God

Next, God prepared Gideon for battle by making it impossible for him to rely on anything or anyone but him. Listen to what the Lord instructs him to do, "You have too many men. When I give you this victory, your men will say, Look what WE did." So, send everyone home who is afraid."

Look at Gideon's raised brow. Still, he turns to his army and says, "Men, if you are the least bit afraid, I relieve you of your duty. Go home."

To Gideon's shock, twenty-two thousand men leave the camp. Still, Gideon and the remainder of his men continue to march toward the enemy camp. But the Lord speaks to Gideon by a brook. "Separate those who lap the water with their tongues like a dog from those who kneel down to drink."

Gideon shakes his head when he sees how many men lay down their weapons and lap the like a dog. By the times he sends this group home, he only has 300 fighting men left. How could *this* be God's provision?

Sometime later, Gideon and his band of three hundred look down on the Valley of Jezeel at the warriors of the enemy's camp swarming like locusts. It's as if we can read his thoughts, *Three hundred men against a hundred thousand men and their camels? Oyvey!*

Before Gideon can bolt, God whispers to Gideon that he will find encouragement at the enemy's outpost. In the dead of night, Gideon and two of his men creep down to the enemy's outpost where they overhear two guards discussing a nightmare. The first guard says, "A loaf of barley rolled into camp and crushed the tents."

The second guard whispers in awe, "This can be nothing other than the sword of Gideon, son of Joash, the Israelite. God has given the Midianites and the whole camp into his hands."

As Gideon makes his way back to camp, he's giddy with encouragement. The enemy expects defeat. *Now*, he's ready for battle.

But let's take a moment to take inventory of what Gideon is bringing into battle:

- Only a handful of soldiers — as directed by God.

- Courage inspired by God.

- God himself.

This is all Gideon needs because he's starting to understand the secret that God's provision is enough.

In the wee hours of the night, Gideon divides his three hundred men into three teams and places them around the upper valley walls surrounding the enemy camp. He gives each warrior a torch, a trumpet, and a jar, but *not* a sword.

On signal, Gideon and his men blow their trumpets, smash their pitchers and shout, "The sword for the Lord and for Gideon"

A very strange thing happens. The Midianites awake to the crashes, trumpet blasts and shouts, they see the torchlight sounding their camp and panic. In the darkness, they sling their swords, but only at one another. Those who survive flee into the mountains, leaving behind one hundred and twenty thousand causalities. What a victory, one God's team won with only a victory cry unto the Lord (Judges 6:33–7:25).

Praise as a Battle Cry

Jack Hayford once said, "Praise is the melody line that will get me in tune with his plan."[39]

I don't know about you, but I'd prefer to follow God's plan over my own. God never loses a battle — if it's HIS battle. If it's our personal battle — a battle outside of God's

[39] Jack Hayford quote from *Living the Way* radio program, "The Power of Heartfelt Song," Pt. 1, May 30, 2006. www.OnePlace.com, © Copyright 2006, Oneplace.com. All rights reserved.

favor, plan, or will—we'll lose the war. There's no enemy God can't conquer when we fight his battle with praise on our lips. So heed Bible teacher, Joyce Meyer's advice when she said, "Stop complaining and start worshipping."[40]

Those of us in ministry know battles often come before ministry events. One summer, when I was a college student, I volunteered as a traveling missionary. My partner, nineteen-year old Lilly and I were bussed around Texas to host vacation Bible schools in a different town every week. Lilly and I soon realized the degree God moved in our VBS meetings was in direct correlation to the degree the enemy attacked us with stress and other nuisances when we arrived into town.

Our greatest attack came in a little town outside El Paso called Faben, the scene of our greatest battle *and* victory.

The church youth group, Lilly my ministry-partner and I had partnered to run the VBS and had been plagued with undercover Satanists. These young men would come into our nightly tent meetings, then afterward, they would lure a member of our group out for a walk. When our member returned, it was as if he would bring a spirit of strife or confusion into our camp. Soon, we had a string of misunderstandings and arguments flaring around us. However one night, as we set around a campfire, we begin to repent of our wrong behaviors. We hugged and forgave one another for all of our backbiting. We also repented to the Lord, and then worshipped him together. The victory was won that night around the campfire. The next day, thirty-eight children came to faith in Jesus in our VBS. It was a true victory.

---

[40] Quote from Joyce Meyer from the CD series *The Battle Belongs to the Lord*, Joyce Meyer Ministries, P.O. Box 655, Felton, MO 63026, www.joycemeyer.org.

A few weeks ago, my husband and I flew to El Paso for a wedding. How surprised I was when we drove to Faben for the rehearsal dinner. I stopped to talk to the restaurant manager. "Thirty years ago, this very week, I was in Faben helping with a Vacation Bible School."

The manager smiled. "I was there. I was one of the children." With tears in his eyes he reached for my hand. "Thank you for coming to tell me about Jesus. That's where I came to faith."

What a moment. It was as if God wrapped me in the warmth of his love to show me the battle was *still* won. The victory was sweeter than ever. We must lay down our own sin, forgive our brothers and sisters, then come to God humbly and seek and worship him. That's the moment when the actual victory is won. The moment worship begins.

Another time, I was rushing to complete the last minute details for a conference when my entire office shut down. In a myriad of what seemed to be unrelated events, I lost my phone, my fax, both printers, and my computer as each piece of my office equipment went dead.

I cried out to God in prayer, "How can I work for you when my office is dead?"

(OOPS! I complained. Complaining is a battle is a strategic no-no.)

Besides, this kind of attack only meant the enemy knew God was on his way to revitalize and renew the hearts of my conference attendees. It was a signal I already had the victory!

As soon as I realized this truth, there was only one thing to do — *praise God*. I shut my office door and begin to sing the old hymns of my childhood. As I did, one by one, my office equipment unexplainably came back to life.

Worshipping Through the Battle

Our destiny, our victory is determined through our worship. It's not about what we deserve, it's about God and our worship walk with him.

But what if we should mess up?

King Jehoshaphat did. He'd followed one of his in-laws, King Ahab, into the wrong battle.

OOPS!

The battle didn't go well and Ahab was killed while Jehoshaphat barely escaped. God expressed his displeasure with Jehoshaphat through a prophet named Jehu, "Should you help the wicked and love those who hate the LORD? Because of this, the wrath of the LORD is upon you." (2 Chron. 19:2)

Basically, Jehoshaphat was finished with God, right?

Wrong.

Though Jehoshaphat displeased God, he sought God for forgiveness and that changed everything. *Let's roll the tape and watch as…*

…Jehoshaphat tears down altars to other gods, turns the people back to the Lord and appoints God-fearing judges and priests to rule over their disputes. But one day, he receives bad news when a young man falls at his feet. "A vast army is coming against you from Edom."

Jehoshaphat wrings his hands. But instead of accepting he was about to get what he deserves, he calls his people together to seek God. A vast crowd gathers in front of the temple and Jehoshaphat stands in front of them, praying and reminding God his people have served God through the generations. He appeals to God's justice as he describes the wrongdoings of his enemy. Then he admits he needs God's help. Let me turn up the volume. "O our God, will you not judge them? For we have no power to face this vast army that is attacking us. We do not know what to do, but our eyes are upon you."

Jehoshaphat could have run to and fro preparing for battle in his own strength, but he's learned this lesson, so he stands and waits on the Lord. In fact, this move was the turning point in the war.

God called a young man named Jahaziel to speak to the people for him, "This is what the LORD says to you: 'Do not be afraid or discouraged because of this vast army. For the battle is not yours, but God's. Tomorrow march down against them. They will be climbing up by the Pass of Ziz, and you will find them at the end of the gorge in the Desert of Jeruel. You will not have to fight this battle. Take up your positions; stand firm and see the deliverance the LORD will give you, O Judah and Jerusalem. Do not be afraid; do not be discouraged. Go out to face them tomorrow, and the LORD will be with you.'"

Let me hit pause while we discuss this. Here's what Jehoshaphat did to restore himself to God and to prepare for battle:

1. He continued to serve God even though he was out of favor.

2. Then, in a time of trouble, he sought God.

3. He called his people to prayer and fasting.

4. He presented his case and appealed to God's sense of justice.

5. He waited on God.

Let's take a look at God's battle plan:

1. Do not be discouraged or afraid—because of the enemy.

2. March against them.

3. Take your positions.

4. Stand firm.

5. Watch the Lord deliver you.

Okay, let's see what happens next...upon hearing God's victory proclamation, Jehoshaphat and his people fall down on their faces and worship God while the priests stand and praise God. The next morning, Jehoshaphat's army prepares to march and Jehoshaphat stands before the throng, "Listen to me, Judah and people of Jerusalem! Have faith in the LORD your God and you will be upheld; have faith in his prophets and you will be successful."

Next, he sends the choir to go before the army. The choir sings, "Give thanks to the LORD, for his love endures forever." As the choir and army marches forward, our camera pans to the battlefield many miles ahead. But the war is already ranging even though Jehoshaphat's army has yet to arrive. What's going on?

Don't you see? The enemy is fighting and killing one another!

By the time Jehoshaphat arrives, the smell of death has already reached his nostrils, before him rests a sea of bodies.

It takes three days to pick up the clothing and equipment left behind. The army of Jehoshaphat worships God all the way home. Once there, they fire up the temple orchestra for an old-fashioned psalm sing.

But why did the victory celebration start even before Jehoshaphat left Jerusalem for war? You heard it yourself from God. *The battle belongs to him.*

So when it came to Jehoshaphat's army, all they could do was take a walk to their enemy's camp and pick up the remaining pieces of a battle they didn't have to fight. All that was left for them to do was to praise God all the way there and all the way home (2 Chronicles 20:1-30).

Jack Hayford says, "If you go about praising, the enemy will run."[41]

This is so true. But even when you are in the middle of a battle you feel you deserve, stop and praise God. Because believe or not, Jesus paid it all so you don't have to.

Story of Paul and Silas

Did Jesus really pay it all? Does God still give the victory when our battle cry is worship?

I've fast-forwarded to Paul and Silas, followers of Jesus who have been thrown in prison for calling on the name of Jesus to heal a demon possessed slave girl. Watch:

It's midnight and Paul and Silas have been beaten and chained in a gloomy, sewage-filled dungeon of a prison. You'd think they'd cry themselves to sleep, but instead, they worship God with prayers and songs until the prison itself begins to shake. An earthquake! As Paul and Silas try to steady themselves, their prison doors fly open and their chains fall away. In fact, all the prisoners are suddenly free.

In the quake, the jailer falls off his cot. Through the swirling dust, he can make out that the prison doors are wide open. He scrambles to his feet and clasps his chest.

---

[41] Jack Hayford quote from *Living the Way* radio program, "Worship Lives," May 19, 2006, www.oneplace.com, © Copyright 2006, Oneplace.com. All rights reserved.

He's a dead man. The Romans will kill him for failing to do his duty. As he draws his sword to kill himself, Paul shouts, "Don't harm yourself! We are all here!"

The jailer freezes and as the dust continues to settle he sees the prisoners are all standing around him. He falls at the feet of Paul and Silas, trembling and asks, "Sirs, what must I do to be saved?"

Paul answers, "Believe in the Lord Jesus, and you will be saved-you and your household."

With great joy, the jailer takes Paul and Silas to his house and washes their wounds and he and all his family are baptized (Acts 16:19-34).

This praising God through the battle appears to be powerful warfare, but what happens when things don't go as you hoped?

1. Trust God anyway.

2. Worship God anyway.

3. Believe all things are working for your good, despite the circumstances – God has more than one way to win a battle.

4. Continue to seek God's direction to make sure you're fighting the right battle. If you're fighting your own battle, give your cause, in its entirety, to God no matter how painful the cost.

5. Know God has not forgotten you. Keep in mind God's perspective is different from yours. The battle is his and your viewpoint of what is happening may be different from the heavenly reality. So rejoice, it's all going to be okay.

6. But in the mean time, stand and wait on the Lord.

Love Notes:

In this chapter we talked about how to:

1. Meet God.
2. Obey God.
3. Repent when you fail him.
4. Inquire of God for direction.
5. Praise him as you wait on him.
6. Be unafraid.
7. Take your position and stand firm.
8. Watch the Lord deliver you.
9. Continue to worship him no matter what.

Worship Experiences:

Experience One:

Contemplate on this name of God:

- **Jehovah-Shalom** (juh-HO-vah shah-LOME) – One use of this name is found in Judges 6:22-24. It's used to describe God who brings us peace. "When Gideon realized that it was the angel of the LORD, he exclaimed, 'Ah, Sovereign LORD! I have seen the angel of the LORD face to face!'

    "But the LORD said to him, 'Peace! (Shalom) Do not be afraid. You are not going to die.'

    "So Gideon built an altar to the LORD there and called it The LORD is Peace (Jehovah-Shalom.)"[42]

    Praise: Jehovah-Shalom, you are the Lord who will provide peace in the middle of my battles. You

---

[42] *The Names of God* Wall Chart.

provided for Gideon by giving him peace over his enemies. You do the same for me. You bring me inner peace through your son, Jesus, who is the Prince of Peace. How can I say thank you for such a gift?

Experience Two:

Let's take Jehoshaphat's story and battle instructions and turn them into a prayer of worship:

Dear Lord,

I seek you. I come to you in prayer and fasting, perhaps by sacrificially denying myself a snack, meal, television, or the Internet.

And I cry out to you, oh Lord, for I have a battle before me. It is: _____. My enemy should not win this battle because it would not honor you because:_____.

(Note: If you can't say this to the Lord, you might not be fighting the right battle.)

Lord, I wait for you. I will not march ahead of you, but I will be still.

(Next, sit quietly before the Lord for a few moments. If God gives you an idea during this time, write it down and determine if this plan is really from God. If it breaks any of the Ten Commandments, it fails the test.)

Continue in prayer:

I will not be discouraged or afraid, because of my enemy; I will trust you, God. I will walk where you lead me as I trust in you. I will obey you, Lord. I will stand firm where you place me and I will wait on you. There I will praise you as I watch you deliver me. I will have faith in the

LORD my God and I will be upheld. I will give thanks to the LORD, for his love endures forever.

In Jesus' Name,

Amen

Experience Three:

Read Psalms 144:1 – 2, as a prayer:

Praise be to the LORD my Rock,
who trains my hands for war,
my fingers for battle.
He is my loving God and my fortress,
my stronghold and my deliverer,
my shield, in whom I take refuge.

Chapter 7

Divine Praise and Laments

Shout for joy to the LORD, all the earth. Worship the LORD with gladness; come before him with joyful songs (Ps 100:1-2).

I recently chatted with my friend Rebekah over a cup of coffee. When she heard I was writing about David, she said, "Can't you just picture him? He had the charisma and likeability of Bill Clinton and the boyish, impulsive charm of Steve Irwin, the Crocodile Hunter."

That could be true! When you consider...

David, the King of Hearts

When the prophet Samuel was led by God to anoint a new King of Israel, he went straight to Bethlehem to visit Jesse, the father of eight sons. As Samuel met each of Jesse's seven eldest, he tried to guess which one God had selected to be king. As they stood before him, Samuel decided God's choice had to be Eliab, the best looking boy of the lot. But Samuel guessed wrong. God told him, "The LORD does not look at the things man looks at. Man looks at the outward appearance, but the LORD looks at the heart" (1 Sam 16:7).

After God nixed each of these seven, Samuel sent for the youngest boy who'd been away tending the family's flock. When David finally ducked into the family home, Samuel was delighted he was a ruddy, handsome young man with a heart for God. Samuel anointed David as the next king right on the spot.

But later, as David matured, he became somewhat of a heartthrob and the subject of a hit song often sung by dancing women:

"Saul has slain his thousands, and David his tens of thousands" 1 Sam 18:7.

Many a woman fell in love with David, including King Saul's daughter Michal, as well as Abigal, Ahinoam, Bathsheba, and dozens more who would become one of his wives or concubines.

But not only was David a ladies' man, he was also brave and daring. As a shepherd boy he'd killed a lion and a bear with his bare hands. Once when visiting his older brothers in King Saul's army, he committed an impulsive, brave act. The Philistine army had faced off against Saul's army and each had camped on either side of a steep gully. Every afternoon Goliath, a giant of a man, would step into the gully and shout up to Saul's army. "Do you need a whole army to settle this? I will represent the Philistines, and you choose someone to represent you, and we will settle this in single combat! If your man is able to kill me, then we will be your slaves. But if I kill him, then you must be our slaves! I defy the armies of Israel! Send me a man who will fight with me" (1 Sam 17:8-10, TLB).

Now this Goliath was a formidable opponent who stood four inches short of a basketball hoop. (That's about nine feet, six inches.) Not only did he have a longer reach with a sword, he wore armor from head to toe. His spear alone weighed about twenty pounds. But these little details didn't intimidate young David. Let's roll the tape so you can see for yourself...

...There's David sauntering down the gully to meet the giant. He's wearing no armor, carries no shield or weapon other than his slingshot, five smooth stones and a deep trust in God. When Goliath jeers at him, David says, "You come against me with sword and spear and javelin, but I come against you in the name of the LORD Almighty, the God of the armies of Israel, whom you have defied. This day the LORD will hand you over to me, and I'll strike you down and cut off your head. Today I will give the carcasses of the Philistine army to the birds of the air and the beasts of the earth, and the whole world will know that there is a God in Israel. All those gathered here will know that it is not by sword or spear that the LORD saves; for the battle is the LORD's, and he will give all of you into our hands" (1 Sam 17:45-47).

While the giant laughs, a single stone springs from David's slingshot and pops Goliath in the middle of his forehead, the only exposed skin not covered by armor. Look at Goliath's stunned expression as he topples to the earth. Without even blinking, David removes Goliath's sword from his hand. He lops off Goliath's head.

David, The King of Praise

Not only was David quite a guy, he was quite a musician, a sort-of rock star in his own right. David's singing was in demand in King Saul's court. Saul had fallen into a deep depression and often summoned the young man to sing a soothing song or two. I'll turn up the volume so you can listen to David's rich voice...

> *I know that the LORD is great, that our Lord is greater than all gods. The LORD does whatever pleases him, in the heavens and on the earth, in the seas and all their depths. He makes clouds rise from the ends of the earth; he sends lightning with the rain and brings out the wind from his storehouses (Psalms 135:5-7).*

But try as David might, he couldn't out-sing the song of jealousy screeching through Saul's heart. The little fact the ladies of the land sang David's praises over Saul's might not have bothered the King so much if he'd retained God's favor. But it was no secret Saul was on the outs with the

Almighty because of his acts of impatience and disobedience. But instead of repentance, Saul chose the way of Cain, apparently believing if he killed God's anointed, he could regain God's favor.

Watch what happens…

…David is in King Saul's court singing as he strums his harp.

ZWOOOMP!

Saul's spear almost pins David to the wall.

You'd think David would part ways with Saul, but he does everything he can to win Saul's favor, defeating two hundred Philistines and even marrying Saul's daughter, Michal. But nothing works…

ZWOOOMP! ZWOOOMP!

David dodges danger twice more.

I'll freeze the picture here. The camera focuses on David's face as it reflects his shock at Saul's murderous rage.

Even though David is now Saul's son-in-law, Saul wants him dead. Only with the help of Saul's daughter and son, Michal and Jonathan, was David able to escape Saul's spear. But David's escape led to a wilderness journey with God, a journey of hardship and trials. While he was on the lam, David fell more deeply in love with God than ever before. He wrote some of his most beautiful songs of praise. David wrote over seventy percent of the songs in the book of Psalms, considered the hymn book of the Hebrews.

Let me turn up David's greatest hit, "The Lord is my Shepherd." It's not the arrangement you may have heard in church. It's played by the temple orchestra with all their many instruments including cymbals, flutes, harps, lyres, and shepherd's pipes. Listen in as the temple choir, about two-hundred-forty-five men and women, sing full voice:

> *The LORD is my shepherd, I shall not be in want.*
> *He makes me lie down in green pastures,*
> *he leads me beside quiet waters,*
> *he restores my soul.*
> *He guides me in paths of righteousness*
> *for his name's sake.*
> *Even though I walk*
> *through the valley of the shadow of death,*
> *I will fear no evil,*
> *for you are with me;*
> *your rod and your staff,*
> *they comfort me.*
> *You prepare a table before me*
> *in the presence of my enemies.*
> *You anoint my head with oil;*
> *my cup overflows.*
> *Surely goodness and love will follow me*
> *all the days of my life,*
> *and I will dwell in the house of the LORD forever.*
> (Psalms 23)

David, The King of Laments

One would think having a heart for God as well as being anointed by God would give one the key to a life of luxury and ease. But this was not the case with young David. No matter the hardship, David grabs his harp and strums his way to worship. Despite David's devotion to God, God did not stop the chase. Saul continued to pursue David and his band of disgruntled tax evaders through the fields of Bethlehem and into the high country and mountain passes.

David often hid in caves, some large enough to hide his entire army of several hundred men. In the caves, or strongholds as David called them he wrote many of his songs of worship, like this one:

> *Have mercy on me, O God, have mercy on me,*
> *for in you my soul takes refuge.*
> *I will take refuge in the shadow of your wings*
> *until the disaster has passed.*
> *I cry out to God Most High, to God,*
> *who fulfills [his purpose] for me.*
> *He sends from heaven and saves me,*
> *rebuking those who hotly pursue me.*
> *God sends his love and his faithfulness.*
> *I am in the midst of lions;*
> *I lie among ravenous beasts —*
> *men whose teeth are spears and arrows,*
> *whose tongues are sharp swords.*
> *Be exalted, O God, above the heavens;*
> *let your glory be over all the earth.*
> *They spread a net for my feet —*
> *I was bowed down in distress.*
> *They dug a pit in my path —*
> *but they have fallen into it themselves.*
> *My heart is steadfast,*
> *O God, my heart is steadfast;*
> *I will sing and make music.*
> *Awake, my soul! Awake, harp and lyre!*
> *I will awaken the dawn.*
> *I will praise you, O Lord, among the nations;*
> *I will sing of you among the peoples.*
> *For great is your love, reaching to the heavens;*
> *your faithfulness reaches to the skies.*
> *Be exalted, O God, above the heavens;*
> *let your glory be over all the earth.*
> (Psalms 57)

I want you to notice something interesting about David's song. It's actually a lament. Matt Redman says, "Apparently about 70 percent of the psalms are laments—in other words, songs of sorrow and crying out. A true lament never challenges or questions the worth of God. Instead, it reveals that His goodness and greatness are the only hope for a bleak situation. Even in our lowest ebb, there should be an underlying trust, and therefore, worship."[43]

A lament can usually be divided into two parts:

Part 1: Alas, all is terrible.

Part 2: Help me Lord, for my hope and trust is in you.

A lament is an act of worship, a faith statement of trust in the face of difficulty. It's a wonderfully honest way to acknowledge our troubles to God as we also acknowledge our hope is in him. It's another way to enjoy a powerful walk with the lover of our souls.

Dr. David Jeremiah's wife was temporarily hospitalized some years ago. Dr. Jeremiah found himself driving around the streets of Fort Wayne, listening to a song called *Through it All*. He said, "It reminded me if we've never had a problem, we'd never know we could trust him. And through those experiences like the one I was experiencing, we'd learn to trust in Jesus."[44]

Here's another great example of a lament from the Psalms, written by David. Pray it as your own prayer:

How long, O LORD? Will you forget me forever?
How long will you hide your face from me?
How long must I wrestle with my thoughts
and every day have sorrow in my heart?
How long will my enemy triumph over me?

---

[43] Matt Redman, *The Unquenchable Worshipper, Coming Back to the Heart of Worship*, P. 27.
[44] Dr. David Jeremiah quote from Turning Point radio broadcast, "Saul's Moods and David's Music, Part One," August 8, 2006, www.oneplace.com, © Copyright 2006, Oneplace.com. All rights reserved.

Look on me and answer, O LORD my God.
Give light to my eyes, or I will sleep in death;
my enemy will say, "I have overcome him,"
and my foes will rejoice when I fall.

But I trust in your unfailing love;
my heart rejoices in your salvation.
I will sing to the LORD,
for he has been good to me.
(Psalm 13)

I'm sure David sang many such laments at his lowest moments. On the lam, he found inspiration for his laments everywhere. I'll queue The God You Need To Know so you can watch what happens when Saul and his army of 3000 approach David's hideout. Saul, not knowing he'd arrived at David lair, steps inside the cave to use it as his private restroom.

David's men, hiding in the shadows, were ecstatic. God delivered Saul into their hands! But that's not how David saw it. He felt he could never slay the man God anointed as king, regardless of the fact David had already been anointed as the next king. So instead of killing Saul, David pulls out his knife and cuts off a piece of Saul's robe. Travel weary Saul doesn't even notice.

Now watch as Saul lumbers back down to his camp with the back of his knees showing. David peers out of the cave, lifting up a swatch of fabric. "Why do you listen to the people who say I am trying to harm you? This very day you have seen it isn't true. For the Lord placed you at my mercy back there in the cave, and some of my men told me to kill you, but I spared you. For I said, 'I will never harm him-he is the Lord's chosen king. See what I have in my hand? It is the hem of your robe! I cut it off, but I didn't kill you! Doesn't this convince you that I am not trying to harm you and that I have not sinned against you, even though you have been hunting for my life?

"The Lord will decide between us. Perhaps he will kill you for what you are trying to do to me, but I will never harm you. As that old proverb says, 'Wicked is as wicked does,' but despite your wickedness, I'll not touch you. And who is the king of Israel trying to catch, anyway? Should he spend his time chasing one who is as worthless as a dead dog or a flea? May the Lord judge as to which of us is right and punish whichever one of us is guilty. He is my lawyer and defender, and he will rescue me from your power" (1 Sam 24:9-15, TLB)!

Saul is stunned. See, he's wiping tears from his eyes. "Is it really you, my son David? You are a better man than I am, for you have repaid me good for evil. Yes, you have been wonderfully kind to me today, for when the Lord delivered me into your hand, you didn't kill me. Who else in all the world would let his enemy get away when he had him in his power? May the Lord reward you well for the kindness you have shown me today. And now I realize that you are surely going to be king, and Israel shall be yours to rule. Oh, swear to me by the Lord that when that happens you will not kill my family and destroy my line of descendants" (1 Sam 24:16-21, TLB)!

David got a reprieve from the wrath of Saul that day, but as usual, that reprieve was short lived. Saul continued to pursue David throughout the land.

David, King of the Hungry

Now David had another problem, not only on the run, he had to take care of a small army and support team of about six hundred. What a responsibility in such a dry land with hunger and thirst as constant companions. So though David was hungering and thirsting for food and water, he was also hungering and thirsting after righteousness. Listen how David worshiped in the sixty-third Psalm:

O God, you are my God,
earnestly I seek you;
my soul thirsts for you,
my body longs for you,
in a dry and weary land
where there is no water (63:1).

David's worship and laments were remarkable in light of his situation. It would be years before the chase would end, before his enemies would be dead, and before he would sit on the throne. Though his journey was difficult, he trusted, worshipped, and walked with God through it all. His difficulties taught him he could really trust God with every problem. God delivered him from his enemies and woes time and again. Though often discouraged, David never gave up on God, That's the reason he's remembered as a man after God's own heart—he sought after it hard.

Read the following Psalm as a prayer:

As the deer pants for streams of water,
so my soul pants for you, O God.
My soul thirsts for God, for the living God.
When can I go and meet with God?
My tears have been my food
day and night.
Why are you downcast, O my soul?
Why so disturbed within me?
Put your hope in God,
for I will yet praise him.
(Psalms 42:1-3, 5, 6)

Love Notes:

In this chapter we talked about trusting God and worshiping him with both praise and laments, as a statement of faith in the midst of difficulty. We've been inspired to seek hard after God, like David, despite our circumstances. We're taking another step forward in our powerful walk with God.

Worship Experiences:

I purposely did not talk about church praise and worship styles in this book. I will say, if you don't like the style of worship in your services, remember:

1.   You are not the one being worshipped.

2.   It's meaningful to worship in a sacrificial way.

Worship is not a matter of pitch, song style, or preference. Worship is a matter of the heart. But good old-fashioned hymn sings have always been part of corporate worship experience. Did you know Moses sang, choirs sang worship songs before a battle, the people sang worship songs in temple, and Jesus sang worship songs at the Last Supper? So, why not you?

Experience One:

A hymn Jesus may have sung with the disciples at the Last Supper is Psalms 113. Read it as a prayer of praise to God:

Praise the LORD.

Praise, O servants of the LORD, praise the name of the LORD.

Let the name of the LORD be praised, both now and forevermore.

From the rising of the sun to the place where it sets, the name of the LORD is to be praised. The LORD is exalted over all the nations, his glory above the heavens.

*Who is like the LORD our God, the One who sits
enthroned on high, who stoops down to look on the
heavens and the earth?*

*He raises the poor from the dust and lifts the needy from
the ash heap; he seats them with princes, with the princes
of their people.*

*He settles the barren woman in her home as a happy
mother of children.*

Praise the LORD. (Psalm 113:1-9)

Experience Two:

Not only did Jesus sing and worship God, so did the
early Christians. Colossians 3:16-17 says, "Let the word of
Christ dwell in you richly as you teach and admonish one
another with all wisdom, and as you sing psalms, hymns
and spiritual songs with gratitude in your hearts to God.
And whatever you do, whether in word or deed, do it all in
the name of the Lord Jesus, giving thanks to God the Father
through him."

Stop here and sing a simple song of praise to God. I
suggest songs from your childhood like "Jesus Loves Me
This I Know," or "God is So Good."

If you don't know any of these songs just sing, "God
loves me. I love God. Thank you Lord!" as best you can in
any melody you know or make one up. Don't worry how it
sounds. No matter how off key you sing, remember, God
loves a joyful noise.

Experience Three:

Dr. David Jeremiah said, "It has become increasingly
popular in our culture for Christians to exempt themselves
from corporate worship. Not only is this unbiblical
(Hebrews 10:24-25), it has the same effect as pulling a log out

of a fire. The personal fire for worship of God burns bright when fueled by the worship of many."[45]

Your next experience is to worship in a corporate (church) worship service as soon as possible.

---

[45] David Jeremiah, "How Can You Life a Lifestyle of Worship", article from www.OnePlace.com, © Copyright 2006, Oneplace.com. All rights reserved.

Chapter 8

Divine Spirit and Truth

"Yet a time is coming and has now come when the true worshipers will worship the Father in spirit and truth, for they are the kind of worshipers the Father seeks" (John 4:23).

I believe walking in a worshipful relationship with God is the very reason for our existence. Jesus himself came to teach us how to worship in spirit and truth. Let's fast-forward through Jesus' early life and watch God's only begotten son grow in wisdom and height…

…He's as a roly-poly toddler in his mother's arms in the markets of Egypt. His family is hiding out from the wrath of King Herod. Next he's in Nazareth, after the death of Herod, playing chase with his brothers and sisters. There's the famous trip he took with his family to the temple. He's accidentally left behind while he was talking to the teachers. Oh, look, there he is with his stepfather Joseph building a table. And there he's calling his disciples.

I'm slowing the footage down to show you Jesus in the city of Sychar, it's an area in Samaria usually avoided by the Jews. As the camera zooms in we see Jesus is resting, leaning against the town's well. He shields his eyes from the sun while a lone figure approaches him.

A woman is lugging her water jug to the well, a rather odd thing to do in the heat of the day. Usually the village women gather in the cool of the morning to draw water and catch up on the latest gossip. But judging from this woman's appearance, she may have reasons to avoid the town gossips.

See how she goes about her business of drawing water, ignoring Jesus. But why not? She knows Jews don't speak to Samaritans, especially Samaritan women. She startles at the sound of his voice.

"Will you give me a drink?"

She lifts her chin to study him. "You are a Jew and I am a Samaritan woman. How can you ask me for a drink?"

Jesus smiles. "If you knew the gift of God and who it is that asks you for a drink, you would have asked him and he would have given you living water."

"Sir, you have nothing to draw with and the well is deep. Where can you get this living water? Are you greater than our father Jacob, who gave us the well and drank from it himself, as did also his sons and his flocks and herds?"

Jesus places his hand on the well's hand-hewn rock. "Everyone who drinks this water will be thirsty again, but whoever drinks the water I give him will never thirst. Indeed, the water I give him will become in him a spring of water welling up to eternal life."

"Sir, give me this water so that I won't get thirsty and have to keep coming here to draw water."

Jesus gestures back toward the village. "Go, call your husband and come back."

She avoids his eyes as she sets her jar down. "I have no husband."

"You are right when you say you have no husband. The fact is, you have had five husbands, and the man you now have is not your husband. What you have just said is quite true."

Her brows arch and her soft brown eyes now focus on his, "Sir, I can see that you are a prophet. Our fathers worshiped on this mountain, but you Jews claim that the place where we must worship is in Jerusalem.

"Believe me, woman, a time is coming when you will worship the Father neither on this mountain nor in Jerusalem. You Samaritans worship what you do not know; we worship what we do know, for salvation is from the Jews. Yet a time is coming and has now come when the true worshipers will worship the Father in spirit and truth, for they are the kind of worshipers the Father seeks. God is spirit, and his worshipers must worship in spirit and in truth."

The woman responds, "I know that Messiah is coming. When he comes, he will explain everything to us."

"I who speak to you am he" (John 4:7-24).

Ah, Jesus, who will speak to even the lowliest of women, *is* the living water. He came to quench our thirst for God. Did you catch that part about worship? Here it is again. Jesus said, "God is spirit, and his worshipers must worship in spirit and in truth."

What does that mean?

To Worship in Spirit

I'm going to rewind to Jesus baptism by John in the Jordon River...

... There's John the Baptist now—he's dressed in camel hair with a leather belt around his waist and he's standing in the river baptizing members of the crowd as he calls them to repentance. He puts his arm around a shivering young man and announces in his booming voice, "After me will come one more powerful than I, the thongs of whose sandals I am not worthy to stoop down and untie. I baptize you with water, but he will baptize you with the Holy Spirit" (Mark 1:7-8).

Jesus watches as John bobs the young man beneath the water. When the young man breaks the surface, Jesus steps out of the crowd and wades into the water. John protests, "I need to be baptized by you, and do you come to me?"

Jesus replies, "Let it be so now; it is proper for us to do this to fulfill all righteousness."

As John baptizes Jesus, God's spirit descends on Jesus like a dove. A voice from heaven says, "This is my Son, whom I love; with him I am well pleased" (Matt 3:11-17).

I'll put our movie on pause as I explain the very day God's spirit rested on Jesus, God's spirit began to lead Jesus. Matthew 4:1 says, "Then Jesus was led by the Spirit into the desert to be tempted by the devil."

Throughout Jesus' earthly ministry, he continued to be led and anointed by God's spirit. For example, at The Lord's Supper, Jesus told those gathered he would soon leave them. Then he told them a great secret, "I have much more to say to you, more than you can now bear. But when he, the Spirit of truth, comes, he will guide you into all truth. He will not speak on his own; he will speak only what he hears, and he will tell you what is yet to come. He will bring glory to me by taking from what is mine and making it known to you" (John 16:12-14).

The spirit of truth would be coming to those Jesus left behind? What was that about? Let's take a moment to visit with Paul to see if we can find out. Now we've met Paul in this Living Story before, but let's take a moment to review. Paul was a latecomer to the faith and not one of Jesus' original disciples. Paul didn't meet Jesus until Jesus died, rose again, and then ascended into heaven. Sometime later Jesus supernaturally appeared on the road to Damascus interrupting Paul's mission to kill Christians. Jesus revealed himself by temporarily striking him blind so Paul could finally see the truth. The encounter opened Paul's spiritually blind eyes and he became a follower of Christ when the very Christians he sought to kill prayed his physical sight would return. And it did!

Paul became a great man of faith. In fact, the letter Paul wrote to his friend Theophilus while under house arrest is now known as The Book of Acts. Let's look over his shoulder as he sits at his desk writing these words...

..."I wrote about all that Jesus began to do and to teach until the day he was taken up to heaven, after giving instructions through the Holy Spirit to the apostles he had chosen. After his suffering, he showed himself to these men and gave many convincing proofs that he was alive. He appeared to them over a period of forty days and spoke about the kingdom of God. On one occasion, while he was eating with them, he gave them this command: 'Do not leave Jerusalem, but wait for the gift my Father promised, which you have heard me speak about. For John baptized with water, but in a few days you will be baptized with the Holy Spirit'" (Acts 1:1-5).

Interesting. Did you know up until this time the Holy Spirit had not rested on, led, or dwelled in the hearts of those who first followed Christ? That is, not until Pentecost. Let's queue up this scene.

...Christ has just been crucified, resurrected, then transcended into heaven and his frightened followers are hiding in the upper room. Suddenly, a loud and mighty wind from heaven blows through the house and tongues of fire rest on each person. The spirit descends on these believers, just as it had descended on Jesus when John baptized him. Ignited by the spirit, the believers are anointed for their first spirit-led task.

Watch as these now fearless believers fly down the stairs and into the streets of Jerusalem. There they encounter Jews, many from out-of-town in order to celebrate the festival of Pentecost. Look at how the believers joyfully share with those in the marketplace. Let's turn up the volume and listen in. *Uh, are they speaking English?*

Not quite, they are speaking in each of the languages represented by the people in the crowd. These believers are preaching about Jesus in languages unknown to them.

Now that's amazing.

Though we don't have to speak in other languages to be led by the spirit, we must be led by the spirit if we want a powerful walk with God.

Be Led By the Spirit

Paul writes what it means to be led by the spirit in Romans 8:13-17 when he said, "For if you live according to the sinful nature, you will die; but if by the Spirit you put to death the misdeeds of the body, you will live, because those who are led by the Spirit of God are sons of God. For you did not receive a spirit that makes you a slave again to fear, but you received the Spirit of sonship. And by him we cry, 'Abba, Father.' The Spirit himself testifies with our spirit that we are God's children. Now if we are children, then we are heirs-heirs of God and co-heirs with Christ, if indeed we share in his sufferings in order that we may also share in his glory."

This beautiful text says the spirit of God leads us out of our chains of fear to become children of God. It also says though we may share in the sufferings of Christ, we will also share in the glory of God.

Paul goes on to describe what living by the spirit looks like, "The fruit of the Spirit is love, joy, peace, patience, kindness, goodness, faithfulness, gentleness, and self-control. Against such things there is no law. Those who belong to Christ Jesus have crucified the sinful nature with its passions and desires. Since we live by the Spirit, let us keep in step with the Spirit. Let us not become conceited, provoking and envying each other" (Gal 5:22-26).

Now, that's a picture I want to resemble!

To Worship in Truth

Jesus taught worship not only in spirit, but in truth. That's interesting because one of the most common quotes of Jesus is the phrase, "I tell you the truth."

Listen to what Jesus told the people when he blessed their children. "*I tell you the truth*, unless you change and become like little children, you will never enter the kingdom of heaven. Therefore, whoever humbles himself like this child is the greatest in the kingdom of heaven" (Matt 18:2-5).

So, the one who called himself truth, taught truth by pointing out he indeed spoke truth. He confirmed this with his disciple Thomas, "Lord, we don't know where you are going, so how can we know the way?"

Jesus replied, "I am the way and the truth and the life. No one comes to the Father except through me" (John 14:5-6).

Listen to what happened when a group of men went to confront Jesus. I'll roll the tape...

...A group of angry men gather around Jesus, "Who are you?"

Jesus eyes fill with love. "Just what I have been claiming all along. I have much to say in judgment of you. But he who sent me is reliable, and what I have heard from him I tell the world."

The men exchange glances, while Jesus continues, "When you have lifted up the Son of Man, then you will know that I am the one I claim to be and that I do nothing on my own but speak just what the Father has taught me. The one who sent me is with me; he has not left me alone, for I always do what pleases him."

Some of the men seemed willing to believe so Jesus continued, "If you hold to my teaching, you are really my disciples. Then you will know the truth, and the truth will set you free (John 8:25-32).

The apostle John, who penned the gospel of John, had this to say about truth, "And the Word became flesh and dwelt among us, full of grace and truth; we have beheld his glory, glory as of the only Son from the Father" (John 1:14, RSV).

To worship God in both spirit and truth means we worship and walk with God, led by and through the spirit, through the truth of the person of Jesus. But there's one more thing, we also need in order to develop a life-style of walking with God in an attitude of worship.

The Right Attitude

Did you know if you get the motions right, but have the wrong attitude, you still blow it? For example, let's pretend you're in a worship service led by King David who seems to only play those same old songs of lament. They're his favorites, but they never seem to edify your spirit. While singing you fume, *You'd think he'd play something more peppy, something I could **really** worship God with, for a change.*

OOPS!

Are you worshipping to edify yourself or to give glory to God? With a right attitude, you can give God glory, even if you don't personally care for the music or lyrics.

First get our attitudes right and dedicate our worship to God and God alone. Though we do benefit from worship because it helps us draw nearer to the Lord, we actually worship for God's benefit—worship is to honor him, not us.

Second we need to stop and see if we have sin in our hearts.

This reminds me of the scene in the movie *The Godfather*.[46] I'll replay it to refresh your memory.

Michael Corleone, following the death of his father, is the head of his mafia family. He's standing piously with the priest at the front of the church as he dedicates himself to God so he can serve as godfather to his infant nephew. But as Michael's words renounce Satan and all his works, his men are carrying out orders to brutally murder the heads of other mafia families.

This is a very eerie scene. And though most of us aren't hit men, we sometimes go through the motions of worship while we carry on with the sin in our hearts. We need to worship with a clean heart because clean temples make better houses of worship. To clean up your act, pray this:

Forgive me Lord. I commit to turn from my sin. Give me your power to help me do so.

In Jesus' name.

We see Jesus explain this concept in the book of Matthew, the twenty-third chapter, where he's once again reprimanding the self-righteousness Pharisees. They were so careful to give the required ten percent to the Lord they'd even given God one tenth of their spices; mint, dill and

---

[46] *The Godfather*, directed by Francis Ford Coppola and starring Marlon Brando, Al Pacino and James Caan, produced by Paramont pictures, 1972, an Albert S. Ruddy Production.

cumin. But this didn't impress Jesus, "You have neglected the more important matters of the law-justice, mercy, and faithfulness. You should have practiced the latter, without neglecting the former. You blind guides! You strain out a gnat but swallow a camel" (23-24).

Gulp!

We have to be careful not to be so overconfident we're righteous in our own eyes alone.

The Blind Can See

But though we see the truth, there are many others who are blind to it. Jesus opened the eyes of a man born blind. The religious leaders called the man before them and demanded to know how he could now see. After much arguing they told him, "Give glory to God, (meaning not to Jesus) we know this man (Jesus) is a sinner."

But the man responded, "Whether he is a sinner or not, I don't know. One thing I do know. I was blind but now I see!"

The religious leaders threw the man out and cancelled his membership with their synagogue. When Jesus heard of it, he went to the man and asked, "Do you believe in the Son of Man?"

"Who is he, sir? Tell me so that I may believe in him."

"You have now seen him; in fact, he is the one speaking with you."

The man fell down and worshiped Jesus. "Lord, I believe."

Jesus replied, "For judgment I have come into this world, so that the blind will see and those who see will become blind" (John 9:24-38).

As the mother of a child considered legally blind, how I delight in this passage. We know Laura has vision loss, but we also know she can see in ways the doctor's can't measure. Recently, one doctor convinced of Laura's blindness, turned his back on her to discuss her case. At the sound of his voice, Laura brightened and began to sing. I told him, "Laura's singing to you."

His eyes widened. He whirled around, knelt beside her wheelchair and, for the first time, made eye contact with my daughter. Laura beamed as she sang him a tuneless song. He *saw* her. "Thank you, Laura." He left the room with spring in his step, a changed man. But the question remains, is Laura blind?

Of course not, she can see love. And so can you. Through the work of Jesus, you can see his great love, grace, and mercy. He has rescued you from sin and death. Won't you join Laura in song?

Love Notes:

In this chapter we talked about walking in the spirit and truth of Jesus. He came to set us free and open our blind eyes.

Worship Experience:

Read or sing the following hymn.

Open My Eyes, That I May See

Open my eyes, that I may see
Glimpses of truth Thou hast for me;
Place in my hands the wonderful key,
That shall unclasp and set me free.
Silently now I wait for Thee,
Ready, my God, Thy will to see;

Open my eyes, illumine me,
Spirit divine!

Open my ears, that I may hear
Voices of truth Thou sendest clear;
And while the wave-notes fall on my ear,
Ev'rything false will disappear.
Silently now I wait for Thee,
Ready, my God, Thy will to see;
Open my ears, illumine me,
Spirit divine!

Open my mouth, and let it bear
Gladly the warm truth ev'rywhere;
Open my heart, and let me prepare
Love with Thy children thus to share.
Silently now I wait for Thee,
Ready, my God, Thy will to see;
Open my heart, illumine me,
Spirit divine!

Clara H. Scott (1841-1897)[47]

---

[47] *Open My Eyes, That I May See* by **Clara** Scott, *The One Year Book of Hymns*, P. Oct 25.

Chapter 9

Divine Plan

"God proved His love on the Cross. When Christ hung, and bled, and died, it was God saying to the world, 'I love you.'" -- Billy Graham[48]

Did you know that the highway of life is actually a toll road? It's true, someone has to pay for our sins, and there are two possibilities, we can try to pay for our sins ourselves, or we can let Jesus Christ pay the toll.

If we choose to pay for our sins ourselves, we'll finally realize we fall short in our efforts to pay the price for our entrance into heaven. Therefore, I hate to say this, but our final destination will be hell. Before you gasp in shock I said that out loud, keep in mind hell is simply the absence of God.

How horrible.

Jesus Paid It All

Let me tell you a story. One dark and icy December night, a trucker at a tollgate flagged me down. He ran to my window and pleaded, "Can you help me, I don't have enough money for the toll." He was in a tight spot. The dollar bill he had in his pocket was not enough to pay the $1.50 toll. He needed six quarters to put into the automated tollbooth and he'd come up short.

This trucker reminds me of us. Not one of us, by our own good works or deeds can pay the toll to eternity with God because we'll come up short every time. No one can pay the toll but Jesus.

---

[48] Billy Graham quote from ThinkExist.com.

Just as I paid the trucker's toll, Jesus paid our toll by his death on the cross. The price of our sin was steep, so steep payment could only be made by the lamb, himself. The only payment pure enough to cover the cost of our sin was his own blood, the blood of deity.

The trucker gave me all he had, his dollar bill in exchange for my six quarters. He had fallen short, but I paid the rest. Trouble was, the trucker couldn't receive my payment until he took it from my open hand. Likewise, we can't receive the payment Jesus made for us until we make change. By "make change" I mean He exchanges our sin for God's mercy and grace. By exchanging our sin for grace, we become true worshippers. Make no mistake; only true worshippers will enter into eternity with God.

That's the deal of a lifetime!

The Passion of Christ

I'm going to hit play on my remote. We're at the turning point of The God You Need To Know. You might recall we lost the right to walk with God in the Garden of Eden. God continued to try to connect with us, through the law (a law we couldn't keep), then animal sacrifices (which were never enough), and finally as a babe in a manger. Could it be? God's son had come to finally save us from our sins so we could be reunited with God?

Before we can answer that question, we must endure the darkest moment in history. The term novelists would refer to as "The Black Moment" of time itself. What comes next may be hard to witness, but don't turn away. Remember, Jesus didn't turn away from you. If the following scenes remind you of the movie, *The Passion of Christ*, know that Gibson's version was actually based on the original.

As we watch these silent images, I will describe what's happening and we'll hear the voice of a narrator reading key

Scriptures describing the action. Note: the passages the narrator reads aren't from the New Testament, (written after the birth of Jesus) these Scriptures are actual prophesies from the Old Testament, also called the Tanak, or the Jewish Bible. These passages were written between two hundred and seven hundred years before Jesus was born…

…This first scene is from the Last Supper. Jesus informed his disciples one of them would betray him. Each asked, "Is it me?" Watch as Jesus dips his bread in the bowl at the same time as Judas. When they make eye contact, Judas knows he's been found out. Judas stands, and then hurries into the darkness to betray the master.

Narrator: Even my close friend, whom I trusted, he who shared my bread, has lifted up his heel against me (Ps 41:9).

Jesus and the remaining disciples go to the Garden of Gethsemane. As Adam was tempted in the Garden of Eden, Jesus is tempted in a garden to abandon the cup of suffering God set before him to drink on our behalf. Instead of walking away, he awaits the arrival of Judas and the soldiers. Judas points out the Master by giving him a kiss. How that must have hurt Jesus to be betrayed by this act of friendship. After the small scuffle between Peter and one of the soldiers, Jesus heals the man's severed ear. Then Jesus allows himself to be led away, held fast between two soldiers.

Narrator: The LORD's anointed, our very life breath, was caught in their traps (Lam 4:20).

Jesus is first brought before the High Priest, the Chief Priest, elders, and teachers of the law. Jesus stands quietly before them while many false witnesses tell wild lies about him, but their lies conflict so formal charges can't be made. Finally someone says, "We heard him say, 'I will destroy this man-made temple and in three days will build another, not made by man.'" But even this testimony doesn't agree with the witnesses.

The high priest asks, "Are you not going to answer? What is this testimony that these men are bringing against you" (Mark 14:60)?

Jesus remains silent.

Then in Mark 14:61, the high priest asks, "Are you the Christ, the Son of the Blessed One?"

"I AM," said Jesus. "And you will see the Son of Man sitting at the right hand of the Mighty One and coming on the clouds of heaven" (62).

The leaders go bezerk. Why? Because Jesus used the name of God, *I AM*. He made himself equal with God.

Shortsighted, they believe Jesus blasphemed God. Now they have legal cause to kill him. In their fury and delight, they blindfold him, pluck his beard, spit on him, beat him, and demand he prophesy who hit him. But he remains silent.

They haul Jesus before the Roman ruler, Pilate. However, Jesus remains silent before his accusers as Pilate asks repeatedly, "Are you the king of the Jews?

Jesus finally says "It is as you say." But then, he would say no more (Mark 15:2-3).

Narrator: He was oppressed and afflicted, yet he did not open his mouth; he was led like a lamb to the slaughter, and as a sheep before her shearers is silent, so he did not open his mouth (Isa 53:7).

Pilate gives in to the Jews and sentences Jesus to death by crucifixion. Jesus silently endures another beating. The soldiers place a purple robe on our master's bloody body and a crown of thorns on his head. They mock, beat, and spit on him. But Jesus remains silent, enduring a brutal flogging.

Narrator: I offered my back to those who beat me, my cheeks to those who pulled out my beard; I did not hide my face from mocking and spitting (Isa 50:6).

The Roman soldiers hand Jesus a heavy wooden cross to carry to Golgotha, the place set aside for crucifixion, but he stumbles.

Narrator: But when I stumbled, they gathered in glee; attackers gathered against me when I was unaware. They slandered me without ceasing. Like the ungodly they maliciously mocked; they gnashed their teeth at me (Ps 35:15-16, KJV).

The soldiers assign a man, Simon, to help him carry his cross up a hill. There they nail Jesus' hands and feet to the cross and raise it into place. The soldiers gamble for his clothes at the foot of the cross. Listen to the narrator describe the crucifixion, reading from a passage by David written before this method of execution was invented.

Narrator: I am poured out like water, and all my bones are out of joint. My heart has turned to wax; it has melted away within me. My strength is dried up like a potsherd, and my tongue sticks to the roof of my mouth; you lay me in the dust of death. Dogs have surrounded me; a band of evil men has encircled me, they have pierced my hands and my feet. I can count all my bones; people stare and gloat over me. They divide my garments among them and cast lots for my clothing (Ps 22:14-18).

They placed Jesus between two criminals and Mark says, "And the inscription of His accusation was written above: THE KING OF THE JEWS. With Him they also crucified two robbers, one on His right and the other on His left. So the Scripture was fulfilled which says, 'And He was numbered with the transgressors.' (Mark 15:26-28 NJKV)

Narrator: Therefore I will give him a portion among the great, and he will divide the spoils with the strong, because he poured out his life unto death, and was numbered with the transgressors (Isa 53:12a).

Darkness fell over the land and Jesus called out, "My God, My God, why have you forsaken Me" (Mark 15:34)? They put vinegar and gall on a sponge and offered it to Jesus, but he refused it.

Narrator: They put gall in my food and gave me vinegar for my thirst (Ps 69:21). It was at that hour, the veil of the temple was torn in two from top to bottom.

Because the Sabbath was fast approaching, and because the officials didn't want to leave bodies hanging on the cross, the Roman soldiers pierced Jesus' side with a spear. Blood and water gushed out as Jesus had already died.

Narrator: Surely he took up our infirmities and carried our sorrows, yet we considered him stricken by God, smitten by him, and afflicted. But he was pierced for our transgressions, he was crushed for our iniquities; the punishment that brought us peace was upon him, and by his wounds we are healed. We all, like sheep, have gone astray, each of us has turned to his own way; and the LORD has laid on him the iniquity of us all (Isa 53:4–6).

In the hush of this moment, I am stunned at how great the sacrifice it was to pay for our souls. I am so amazed at the detail of the fulfilled prophecies and of Jesus' great mission carried out in love. Joseph of Arimathea, a prominent and rich man, came to take Jesus' body and place it in his own tomb.

Narrator: He was assigned a grave with the wicked, and with the rich in his death, though he had done no violence, nor was any deceit in his mouth (Isaiah 53:9).

Still, why did he do it? Why did he die, like that, for us?

Narrator: Yet it was the LORD's will to crush him and cause him to suffer, and though the LORD makes his life a guilt offering, he will see his offspring and prolong his days, and the will of the LORD will prosper in his hand. After the suffering of his soul, he will see the light [of life] and be satisfied; by his knowledge my righteous servant will justify many, and he will bear their iniquities. ...For he bore the sin of many, and made intercession for the transgressors (Isaiah 53:10-12b).

A Billion To One

Jesus bore our sins. We are justified through him.

Some time ago I helped narrate a Denver Celebration TV show with Alan Huth from the Ezra Project, a ministry by which connects God's people to God's word. Alan and I read many of the correlating Scriptures from both the Old Testament and New Testament describing the birth, life, death and resurrection of Jesus. As we discussed the incredible prophecies and their fulfillment, I said, "If I were going to try to deceive people by studying prophecy, then try to fulfill it, I wouldn't pick these kinds of prophecies that required beating, spitting, plucking out my beard, or crucifixion. I would be more about sitting on a throne."

Alan agreed.

In the book I wrote with William (Bill) Fay, Share Jesus Without Fear, Bill tells a story about talking to a waiter about the chance of so many Biblical prophecies coming true. He asked Art, "What is a penny doubled every day for thirty days."

Art answered, "It starts out at 1, 2, 4, 8. 16, 32, 64. 128, 245 until you get to $10,737,418.24."

Bill then asked, "How many people would it take flipping quarters until one person hit heads thirty times in a row?"

Art's answer was billions of people.

"Art's right. According to *Ripley's Believe it or Not! Strange Coincidences*, for a tossed coin to fall to heads fifty times in a row, would require one million men tossing ten coins a minute for forty hours a week – and then it would only occur once in every nine centuries."

Bill then explained that was why he believed the Bible to be true. He said, "If you take the thirty prophecies about the birth, death, the resurrection of Jesus that have come true, that's like flipping heads thirty times in a row." Bill then asked, "How many times would it take for a person to flip a quarter before he hit heads 245 times? I pick that number because it's a conservative estimate of the biblical prophecies that were supposed to have come true that have come true."[49]

What are the odds? By conservative estimates, the odds are a billion-to-one.

Our Redeemer

Jesus didn't come as an earthly king but to be our redeemer; in fact Redeemer (Job 19:25) is one of the many names of Jesus. What is a redeemer exactly? A redeemer is someone, usually a relative, who pays a great price to purchase a person from slavery.[50] Jesus is called the

[49] William Fay and Linda Evans Shepherd, Share Jesus Without Fear, (Nashville, TN: Broadman and Holman Publishers, 1999) P. 89-90.
[50] Berkeley & Alvera Mickelsen, *The Family Bible Encyclopedia Volume Two* (Colorado Springs, CO: David C. Cook Publishing Company, 1978), P. 114.

Redeemer because he redeemed us from sin by dying on the cross for us. Because he paid the price we can walk with God. Billy Graham once said, "No man ever loved like Jesus. He taught the blind to see and the dumb to speak. He died on the cross to save us. He bore our sins. And now God says, 'Because He did, I can forgive you.'"

I want to share a story that describes what Jesus did for us.

My husband Paul, whom I've nicknamed My Hero, is a man who loves the outdoors. He mountain bikes, skis downhill, and has climbed all fifty-two fourteen-thousand-foot peaks in the state of Colorado, something only a few people have ever accomplished.

On one particular climb, just outside of Aspen, Paul and two of his friends were climbing the Maroon Bells, two rugged hunks of granite that jut out of the earth. These two fourteen-thousand-foot peaks are connected only by a narrow knife-ridge of rock.

Where was I? I was back in the Aspen hotel room, praying everyone would have a safe journey. I had many reasons to worry, but one was something that happens every afternoon here in Colorado; *lightning*! When climbing in the Colorado high country, you have to start early (like 2:00 am) so you can get off a peak before the afternoon thunderstorms.

Paul and our friends climbed to the top of the first Maroon Bell by noon. The clouds were already rolling in. As Paul's party tried to traverse the knife ridge connecting the two peaks, they came to a gap in the ridge, a deep crevasse. My husband and his friend John were able to step across it. But John's wife, Cindy, did exactly what I would have done. She sat down and cried.

That's when my husband completed a picture of what Jesus did for us. Paul actually climbed down into the gap. With only air beneath him, he stretched out his arms and legs to touch each side of the gap walls. He held himself in place while Cindy walked across his shoulders.

What a man!

Isn't that what Christ did for us? He stood on the cross, bridging the gap between God and man, so we could walk across his shoulders to God.

Our Life is but a Vapor

If you haven't already, decide what you are going to do with Jesus. However, by choosing not to decide, realize you've decided not to follow him. If this describes your choice, "Good luck," and as Bill Fay would say, "Please drive carefully."

In the movie *The Corpse Bride*, the Black Widow Spider brought this point home. She sang a ditty reminding us life is just a "temporary state" and she's absolutely right—life is temporary but eternity lasts forever.[51]

I once read about a trial where a witness was asked if he knew the deceased before or after he died. Now, that's funny! But similar to a question we'll all be asked on judgment day. The Lord will want to know, "Were you acquainted with my son, Jesus, before or after you died?"

We can wait until it's too late. Instead of knowing him as our savior in this life, we can get to know him as our judge in the life to come.

---

[51] Reference from Tim Burton's *The Corpse Bride* © 2005 Warner Brother's Entertainment Inc. http://www.imdb.com/title/tt0121164/quotes.

The Key

One day a friend of mine tried to open her car door by pressing the button on her electric key, but the process failed. She manually unlocked her door with the key. But the real problem occurred when she put the key in the ignition. Not only would the car not start, the alarm sounded. The reason? The battery in the electronic key was dead. The key still fit the lock but there was no spark of recognition.

This is an example for us. We may know all about Jesus, sung worship songs, be able to quote the Bible forwards and backwards, and still not be true worshippers because we've never walked with God. Then when judgment day comes, we could hear God say to us, *"I never knew you."*

I want to not only recognize God; I want him to recognize me. But more than that, I want to walk with him. That will only happen when I recognize Jesus, ask him to forgive me for my sins, then walk with God as led by the spirit. As we become true worshippers, we will not only recognize God, he will recognize us. We will walk together, hand in hand.

You can know about Him or you can know him. No cause for alarm; it's that spark of recognition that makes the difference.

Love Notes:

In this chapter we talked about:

- God loved us so much, he sent his son to die in our place.

- This was no accident, and was foretold in detail by God's prophets, hundreds of years before it happened.

- It's not enough to know and understand The God You Need To Know, we must ask God to forgive us through the sacrifice of Jesus, turn from our sins, and walk with Jesus— following him by the power of the Holy Spirit.

Worship Experience:

Experience One:

Contemplate on some of the names of Jesus.

- Messiah – is translated from the Hebrew into the Greek as Christ. It means "Anointed One." Jesus is the messiah.

- Savior – seeks to save that which was lost. Jesus is our Savior.

- Master – Jesus is our master, our teacher, our rabbi. He is the only one who can point us to God so that we can walk with him.

- Redeemer – Christ death paid our debt for sin. Jesus has bought us from the bondage of sin. Jesus is our Redeemer.

- Son of God – Jesus is the only begotten Son of God, meaning he was born of a virgin. He came from God, to become a man, so we could have life through him. Jesus is the Son of God.[52]

Experience Two:

Read or sing the following hymn.

---

[52] *The Names of Jesus* pamphlet, Torrance, CA: RW Research Inc. Rose Publishing Inc., 2006).

When I Survey the Wondrous Cross

When I survey the wondrous cross
On which the Prince of glory died,
My richest gain I count but loss,
And pour contempt on all my pride.
Forbid it, Lord, that I should boast,
Save in the death of Christ, my God;
All the vain things that charm me most--
I sacrifice them to His blood.
See, from His head, His hands, His feet,
Sorrow and love flow mingled down;
Did e'er such love and sorrow meet,
Or thorns compose so rich a crown?
Were the whole realm of nature mine,
That were a present far too small:
Love so amazing, so divine,
Demands my soul, my life, my all.

Isaac Watts (1674-1748)[53]

---

[53] *When I Survey the Wondrous Cross* by Isaac Watts from *The One Year Book of Hymns*, April 5.

Chapter 10

Divine Living

He's no fool who gives up what he cannot keep to gain what he cannot lose. – Jim Elliot[54]

We just left the Black Moment of time itself when our Master, Jesus Christ, was crucified on the cross. But that's not the end of the story. It's the turning point in the great romance between God and man. It's the moment before man is able to finally worship his creator in a daily walk. Let's press play to see what happens next…

…The music is somber because Jesus is dead. Darkness has fallen over the land though only the mid-afternoon as if all creation is mourning. The women weep as the soldiers remove Christ's body from the cross.

Enter a follower of Jesus from Arimathea. You can tell by his robes that Joseph is a rich man. He has special permission to take Jesus' body to his own tomb before sunset.

Joseph and a man helping him, carry our Lord's body to a tomb carved from a hillside. Its entrance is covered by a heavy, flat, wheel-like rock. Joseph rolls away the stone then he and his helper carefully lay the body of Jesus inside. Joseph wraps the body in strips of cloth. Then as customary, anoints the body with pounds of spices to delay the stench of death.

When Joseph finishes, the tomb is sealed while the women—Mary Magdalene and the other Mary, sit by the tomb and sob. The two women are not alone at the gravesite.

---

[54] Jim Elliot quote, JesusSite.com

For at the request of the Pharisees, Pilate sent Roman guards to make sure the disciples don't come to steal Jesus' body.

Three days later, guards still stand at the tomb's entrance, the hush of morning yawns into sunrise. An earthquake shivers the trees and causes a spray of rocks to tumble down the hillside. Rays of white light, brighter than the dawn, spill from the cracks in the tomb's seal. The soldiers watch in amazement as a dazzling angel rolls away the stone. The figure of a man wrapped in bloodstained burial clothes slowly stands upright. With help from the angel, the shrouded figure, his eyes gleaming with life, removes the burial cloth from his face as the trembling soldiers faint.

In this next scene, we see Mary Magdalene and the other Mary arrive to check on the tomb. See their shock to discover the soldiers are gone and the stone's been rolled away. Has Jesus' body been moved? Where?

When they look inside the tomb they see an angel, " Do not be afraid, for I know that you are looking for Jesus, who was crucified. He is not here; he has risen, just as he said. Come and see the place where he lay. Then go quickly and tell his disciples: 'He has risen from the dead and is going ahead of you into Galilee. There you will see him.' Now I have told you" (Matt 28:5-7).

The women enter the tomb. It smells of spices and they see the burial clothes neatly folded. That's when it hits them. No one would remove a rotting body and leave the burial clothes behind. By this point the bandages held back the stench and kept the body intact. Plus, how could one explain the presence and message of the angel?

The women are filled with joy and run to tell the disciples. On their way, the women see a man who calls them by name— Jesus! They fall at his feet to worship him.

He says, "Do not be afraid. Go and tell my brothers to go to Galilee; there they will see me" (Matt 28:10).

The women race to share the news. Magdalene arrives first, and in her joy, she calls out to the men, "I have seen the Lord" (John 20:18)!

It's a new dawn as the dark night of man's separation from God is over. Jesus is risen, and in so doing, defeated both sin and death. He fulfilled the law <u>and</u> the prophecies. He broke the curse of the Garden of Eden by reuniting man with his creator.

Resurrected Living

Have you seen Jesus? Like the two women, have you fallen down and worshipped him? How should that change your life?

My friend's mother is in her nineties and has a collection of blouses decades old. "They have a lot of wear left," she insists. Maybe, but because of her poor eyesight she can't see these old blouses are covered with stains and spots. I think we often see ourselves in "soft focus" and somehow overlook the stains and spots of our sin. We can't walk with God covered in such filth. God's given us the righteousness (or purity) of Christ. But now, we can wash our dirty robes in his blood so we can appear before him blameless and without spot.

But how then shall we live? Are we free to sin abundantly? Personally, I think you'll reconsider that choice if you truly love Christ. Because it's your love for him that motivates you to walk the walk of the righteous. I like to think of it like this—if I continue in my sin, have I added to the suffering of Christ?

A stunning thought that makes me want to be a better person. Paul said in the book of Romans, "Therefore, I urge you, brothers, in view of God's mercy, to offer your bodies as living sacrifices, holy and pleasing to God-this is your spiritual act of worship" (12:1).

What is a Living Sacrifice?

A visitor to our website GodTest.com, wrote to say, "You have shown me Jesus. I know now there is hope. I was searching the Internet for ways to kill myself when your page came up. And as I followed each link, I found the answer. It was hard for me to give my life to Jesus; I felt as though something inside me was blocking my heart and mouth from saying the words. I know now it was the devil holding me back and it was God who helped pull me through. Thank you from my newborn heart."

The writer's correct. It's a hard decision to follow Christ. It's difficult because following Christ is a commitment. Are you ready to commit the whole of your person to be a living sacrifice to God? While though it's true we can freely come to God through Christ, we cannot freely live for God. The walk comes at a price—a price where we give *all* of ourselves to live as a sacrifice to God.

How to Live as a Sacrifice

This morning, I made a decision. I decided I would be honest with you about what it cost me to write this book. To explain the cost, let me tell you what happened. One day, many years ago, I walked across the tradeshow floor at the bookseller's convention. Excited, I had an appointment with a well-known editor at a large publishing house. I hoped to pitch him an idea for a project But when I arrived at the appointment, "Sam" pulled me aside and asked, "Why are you even here?"

My heart sank. "Pardon me?"

"I've watched you over the years," Sam said, "and I know how much hurt and betrayal you've endured in publishing. If I were you, I'd quit. I'd go home and work in my home church and teach Sunday school. I mean, why beat yourself up?"

"Sam," I said, "I would love to quit. But that's not what God's called me to do. I motioned to the thousands upon thousands of new books and gift products that encircled us. "God's called me to be here. And yes, it has been a difficult journey, but no matter the cost, I have to be obedient. Even if I never publish another book, even if I'm betrayed in every publishing experience, I have to be where God has called me. Where else would I go?"

Sam shook his head, possibly feeling sorry for me and possibly believing I'd truly lost my marbles. But what Sam didn't know is every year I seek God on this very issue, waiting on him until I feel satisfied he's answered my plea. "Lord, take this cup from me. I will follow you and obey your will." Every year, I pray until I have peace I am still on the right path – I know for a certainty what I am supposed to do, I am to write.

That doesn't mean my journey has been easy, nor does it mean it's only been difficult or without reward. I've enjoyed the sweet fellowship of God and those he has sent into my life. I'd do it all over again if for no other reason but to walk with God. Like David, I've walked with God though difficulty, and in the process learned God is a God I can trust. I know because this book you're now reading has been particularly difficult. Satan has tried repeatedly to kill the project. First, the manuscript had to be recreated after a computer crash. Then when my signed publisher changed editors, the new editor told me she hated this book and canceled my contract. She advised me I should never write again. Following that, my then agent severed our relationship. Other publishers not only rejected this book, my favorite publisher rejected it four times. But still, God called me to press on. And now, after years of delay, it's not a coincidence this book is in your hands. In God's perfect timing, it's right where he called it to be in this very moment.

Was it worth it? No question. In fact, I'd do it all over again.

But back to the question about the revelation of Christ. How then shall we live? Paul, in Ephesians 5, has some great advice:

> Be very careful, then, how you live-not as unwise but as wise, making the most of every opportunity, because the days are evil. Therefore do not be foolish, but understand what the Lord's will is. Do not get drunk on wine, which leads to debauchery. Instead, be filled with the Spirit. Speak to one another with psalms, hymns, and spiritual songs. Sing and make music in your heart to the Lord, always giving thanks to God the Father for everything, in the name of our Lord Jesus Christ.
>
> Submit to one another out of reverence for Christ.
>
> Wives, submit to your husbands as to the Lord. For the husband is the head of the wife as Christ is the head of the church, his body, of which he is the Savior. Now as the church submits to Christ, so also wives should submit to their husbands in everything.
>
> Husbands, love your wives, just as Christ loved the church and gave himself up for her to make her holy, cleansing her by the washing with water through the word, and to present her to himself as a

radiant church, without stain or wrinkle or any other blemish, but holy and blameless. In this same way, husbands ought to love their wives as their own bodies (15-29).

Everyone gets hung up on the part where wives are supposed to submit to their husbands, but did you catch the part where we are to submit to one another, and the part where husbands are supposed to LOVE their wives. Make no mistake, this is a balanced teaching and should never be used to control the actions of others. Love would never do that.

But keep in mind, we're not perfect and neither was Paul. He wrote in Romans 7:14-23.

The law is good, then, and the trouble is not there but with me because I am sold into slavery with Sin as my owner.

I don't understand myself at all, for I really want to do what is right, but I can't. I do what I don't want to- what I hate. I know perfectly well that what I am doing is wrong, and my bad conscience proves that I agree with these laws I am breaking. But I can't help myself because I'm no longer doing it. It is sin inside me that is stronger than I am that makes me do these evil things.

I know I am rotten through and through so far as my old sinful nature is concerned. No matter which way I turn I can't make myself do right. I want to but I can't. When I want to do good, I don't; and when I try not to do wrong, I do it anyway. Now if I am doing what I don't want to, it is plain where the trouble is: sin still has me in its evil grasp.

It seems to be a fact of life that when I want to do what is right, I inevitably do what is wrong. I love to do God's will so far as my new nature is concerned; but there is something else deep within me, in my lower nature, that is at war with my mind and wins the fight and makes me a slave to the sin that is still within me. In my mind I want to be God's willing servant, but instead I find myself still enslaved to sin.

So you see how it is: my new life tells me to do right, but the old nature that is still inside me loves to sin. Oh, what a terrible predicament I'm in! Who will free me from my slavery to this deadly lower nature? Thank God! It has been done by Jesus Christ our Lord. He has set me free (TLB).

You and I and Paul, we ALL need a savior. For try as we might, none of us are perfect. This fact leads us back to grace, as Paul also said, "For it is by grace you have been saved, through faith-and this not from yourselves, it is the gift of God- not by works, so that no one can boast. For we are God's workmanship, created in Christ Jesus to do good works, which God prepared in advance for us to do" (Eph 2:8-10).

Therefore, we live for Christ, we do our best in his power and strength, doing the good works God has prepared for us to do.

Why the World Hates Us

To answer the question, "Why does the world hate us," we don't have to go any further than the words of Jesus, "All men will hate you because of me" (Luke 21:17).

Why does the world hate Jesus? He tells us in John 7, "It hates me because I testify that what it does is evil" (7). The world is evil and hates those who try to do good. This is one of the reasons why we are losing seventy percent of young believers after they enter institutions of higher learning. The world of campus life, peers, and professors are teaching our children to worship immorality.

I received a call from a college student who'd been ostracized by her suitemates when they found a Bible on her bed. "We didn't know you were a Christian," they said. "We don't want to have anything to do with you." She wept as she told me she's no longer included in their conversations.

Another student was told by his professor on the first day of class, "If you are a Christian, you might as well un-enroll from my class now, because I'll never pass you."

Wow, it's rough out there.

What should our response be when we face this kind of persecution? James tells us, "Dear brothers, is your life full of difficulties and temptations? Then be happy, for when the way is rough, your patience has a chance to grow. So let it grow, and don't try to squirm out of your problems. For when your patience is finally in full bloom, then you will be ready for anything, strong in character, full and complete (James 1:2-4, TLB).

Our Response to the World

I had dozens of light bulbs in my kitchen going out, one-by-one, for months. Not that I noticed, until the last light bulb blinked out and my family and I were left in the dark. Whoa, what a difference that last light bulb made.

You may think the light you shine into the darkness makes no difference. That's not so. Matt 5:16 says, "Let your light shine before men, that they may see your good deeds and praise your Father in heaven."

This reminds me of the little girl who asked, "Mom, is God is bigger than me?"

"Yes!"

"And he lives inside me?"

"Oh, yes!"

The little girl looked down at herself. "Does He shine through the cracks?"

I love this visual. It reminds me God's love shines through my cracks so others will be drawn to him. Remember, the world is the same place as it was when Christ came and rescued us. We need to love others who are still a part of this world and to desperately pray for our generation. What do we pray? We pray for mercy and grace. We pray for repentance, and repentance starts with us.

Love Notes:

In this chapter we talked about:

- The resurrection of Jesus.

- How to resurrect our own lives by living as a living sacrifice.

- How to shine for Christ.

- The way is not always easy, but it's worth a chance to walk with God.

- We learn God is a God we can trust because of our difficulties.

Worship Experience:

Experience One:

As a prayer of repentance, read Psalms 51. Note: this is the prayer David wrote after he committed adultery with Bathsheba then had her husband murdered when he learned she was pregnant.

Have mercy on me, O God, according to your unfailing love; according to your great compassion blot out my transgressions. Wash away all my iniquity and cleanse me from my sin.

For I know my transgressions, and my sin is always before me. Against you, you only, have I sinned and done what is evil in your sight, so that you are proved right when you speak and justified when you judge. Surely I was sinful at birth, sinful from the time my mother conceived me. Surely you desire truth in the inner parts; you teach me wisdom in the inmost place.

Cleanse me with hyssop, and I will be clean; wash me, and I will be whiter than snow. Let me hear joy and gladness; let the bones you have crushed rejoice. Hide your face from my sins and blot out all my iniquity.

Create in me a pure heart, O God, and renew a steadfast spirit within me. Do not cast me from your presence or take your Holy Spirit from me. Restore to me the joy of your salvation and grant me a willing spirit, to sustain me.

Then I will teach transgressors your ways, and sinners will turn back to you. Save me from bloodguilt, O God, the God who saves me, and my tongue will sing of your righteousness. O Lord, open my lips, and my mouth will declare your praise. You do not delight in sacrifice, or I would bring it; you do not take pleasure in burnt offerings. The sacrifices of God are a broken spirit; a broken and contrite heart, O God, you will not despise.

In your good pleasure make Zion prosper; build up the walls of Jerusalem. Then there will be righteous sacrifices, whole burnt offerings to delight you; then bulls will be offered on your altar.

Experience Two:

Read or sing the old hymn, as a prayer:

Blessed Assurance

Blessed assurance, Jesus is mine!
O what a foretaste of glory divine!
Heir of salvation, purchase of God,
Born of His spirit, washed in His blood.
This is my story, this is my song,
Praising my Savior all the day long;
This is my story, this is my song,
Praising my Savior all the day long.

Perfect submission, perfect delight!
Visions of rapture now burst on my sight;
Angels descending bring from above
Echoes of mercy, whispers of love.
Perfect submission--all is at rest,
I in my Savior am happy and blest;
Watching and waiting, looking above,
Filled with His goodness, lost in His love.

Fanny Jane Crosby (1820-1915)[55]

---

[55] *Blessed Assurance* by Fanny Jane Crosby from *Great Songs of the Church Number Two*, P. 21.

Chapter 11

Divine Savior

He (Christ) is the Head of the body made up of his people-that is, his Church-which he began; and he is the Leader of all those who arise from the dead, so that he is first in everything; for God wanted all of himself to be in his Son (Col 1:18-19, TLB).

So often we see Jesus as our *personal* savior, as in personal chef or personal assistant, or as someone committed to *serving* us. Our vision of Jesus is so small it's ridiculous. Yes, we can have a personal relationship with Jesus, but we need to expand our understanding of who he is. When we start to see the glorified Jesus, we will fall to our knees to worship. We will have no choice.

One of the best places to see Jesus in his glory is the book of Revelation where the apostle John describes his vision. Though we also see visions of Jesus peeking out of the pages of Daniel and Isaiah, as well as other Old Testament books. These visions of our Lord are remarkably similar, holy, and breathtaking. Every person who spoke of such a vision relayed the same response, an encounter with the glorified Christ brings them to their knees.

Background of the Book

The book of Revelation was probably written some sixty-plus years after the resurrection of Jesus. The church was under great persecution and John, who was now an old man, had been banished by the Roman emperor to the Isle of Patmos.

While imprisoned on the island, John received a vision of the glorified Jesus. This vision included mysterious prophecies about the End of Days, as well as a message from

Jesus to the churches. John put the impressions of his heavenly vision, plus the words given by Jesus, onto papyrus.

As we discuss what John says, note Revelations is the only book in the Bible that comes with a blessing to those who study it and a curse to those who alter it. This is a book of mystery, written in code. One of this book's wonders is you can reference every section to prophecy found elsewhere in the Bible, including the Old Testament. How remarkable is that?

I cannot explain all the mysteries of this book, but I can show you how Jesus reveals himself in his glory, what he says to us, his church, and how he wants to be worshipped.

John's Vision of Jesus

The last time John saw Jesus was forty days after Jesus' resurrection from the dead. Jesus had been John's dearest friend. John leaned on Jesus during the Lord's Supper. I don't think he was prepared to see Jesus in his glorified state. Would you expect to see your best friend as God?...

...John hears a loud voice like a trumpet, "Write on a scroll what you see and send it to the seven churches: Ephesus, Smyrna, Pergamum, Thyatira, Sardis, Philadelphia, and Laodicea."

John turns to see who is speaking to him, and sees seven golden lamp stands. There's someone, "like the Son of Man", walking through the stands. He's dressed in a robe reaching down to his feet and has a golden sash around his chest. His head and hair are white like lamb's wool, as white as snow. His eyes are like blazing fire. His feet are like bronze glowing in a furnace, and his voice is like the sound of rushing waters. He holds seven stars in his right hand and his mouth contains a sharp double-edged sword. His face is like the sun shining in all its brilliance.

Pause scene. What a vision! This is a far cry as to how we often see Jesus depicted in some of our modern churches, still hanging on a cross. Not only has Jesus risen, he's in his glory. I'll take our movie off of pause…

…As soon as John sees the resurrected Christ, he falls down as though he were dead. Jesus reaches out with his right hand and touches him. "Do not be afraid. I am the First and the Last. I am the Living One; I was dead, and behold I am alive forever and ever! And I hold the keys of death and Hades" (Rev 1:9-18).

I'm going to flip through my Bible and show you another picture of Jesus, as told to by Daniel, a prophet from the Old Testament who lived about six-hundred-and-fifty years before Jesus was born as a babe in the manger.

Daniel explains, "As I was standing on the bank of the great river, the Tigris, I looked up and there before me was a man dressed in linen, with a belt of the finest gold around his waist. His body was like chrysolite, his face like lightning, his eyes like flaming torches, his arms and legs like the gleam of burnished bronze, and his voice like the sound of a multitude" (Dan 10:4-6).

Notice any similarities? Like John, Daniel fell before this vision like one dead. Like John, he was physically touched by the messenger and was told to listen. A lot of people will tell you this being Daniel saw was an angel, and that's true. An angel is *one sent by God*. But could this *one sent by God* be Jesus? I think so, besides this messenger was speaking parts of the same revelation as John.

There are other documented descriptions of Jesus as told to us by the Old Testament prophets. Let's continue to study John's encounter with Jesus because it holds the key to deeper worship. Jesus told him…

..."Write, therefore, what you have seen, what is now and what will take place later. The mystery of the seven stars that you saw in my right hand and of the seven golden lamp stands is this: The seven stars are the angels of the seven churches, and the seven lamp stands are the seven churches" (Rev 1:19-20).

After this, Jesus lays out a message for the seven churches. In some ways he's giving each church a report card. You can go back and read the exact text later (Rev. 2:1 – 3:22,) for now we are going to view his message as though it were a report card.

But before we get started, did you know God specified the Israelites place seven lamp stands before the Ark of the Covenant in the tabernacle and the temple's Holy of Holies? This is amazing and tells us God wants to fill his churches with his presence.

Church Report Card

This report card is most interesting and is given to seven types of churches. Study it to see which of these churches are passing and which are failing, and why. See what the rewards will be to the churches that overcome. Check to see what kind of church you represent or attend. Pray God will give you wisdom to help you and your church pass their test.

Church 1: The Church of Ephesus

- **Grade:** Not yet passing.

- **Successes:** Jesus commends them for good deeds and hard work, perseverance, not allowing sin into their fellowship, testing teachers to make sure they're true, enduring hardships in Jesus name, not growing weary, and also for hating the evil practices of the Nicolaitans– which encouraged Christians to freely indulge in sin under the cover of grace.

- **Problems:** Left their first love—their love and passion for Christ.

- **How to Improve:** Repent and do the things you first did or you will have your lamp stand removed.

- **Reward if Overcomes:** Jesus will give them the right to eat from the tree of life in the paradise of God (Rev 2:1-7).

Church 2: *The Church of Smyrna*

- **Grade:** Passing

- **Successes:** They are rich because they are enduring afflictions, slander, and poverty.

- **Problems:** They have an upcoming test of persecution.

- **To Improve:** Continue to be faithful to the point of death.

- **Reward if Overcomes:** Will have the crown of life (Rev 2:8-11).

Church 3: *The Church of Pergamum*

- **Grade:** Some members passing, others failing.

- **Successes:** They remained true to Jesus' name and did not renounce their faith when their friend was put to death.

- **Problems:** They allow those into their fellowship who hold to false teachings (allowing the eating of meat offered to false idols and sexual immorality as well as the false doctrines of the Nicolaitans).

- **To Improve:** The church should repent or Jesus will come to fight them (false teachers) with the sword of his mouth.

- **Reward if Overcomes:** Jesus will give them some of the hidden manna. He will also give them a white stone with a new and secret name written on it (Rev 2:12-17).

Church 4: The Church of Thyatira

- **Grade:** Some members passing, others failing.

- **Successes:** Jesus knows their deeds, love, faith, service, and perseverance and they are doing even more than they did at first.

- **Problems:** The church tolerates a type of Jezebel, a woman who calls herself a prophetess. Her teachings lead the people to eat food sacrificed to idols and to sexual immorality.

- **To Improve:** Because the Jezebel did not take the chances God gave her, she will suffer and her children will die. Her students will also suffer until they repent. Those who do not follow her teachings will not suffer. This group is to hold on to their faith.

- **Reward if Overcomes** (and does his will until the end): Jesus will give them authority over the nations as he received authority from his Father. He will also give them the morning star (Rev 2:18-29).

Church 5: The Church of Sardis

- **Grade:** Most in the church are failing.

- **Successes:** A few have not soiled their clothes (sinful living) and are worthy.

- **Problems:** They have a reputation for being alive but they are dead.

- **To Improve:** Strengthen what remains, and is about to die, by remembering what they've learned in the past, obeying these teachings, and repenting. If they don't wake up, Jesus will come to them like a thief.

- **Reward if Overcomes:** He will dress them in white and never blot out their name from the Book of Life, but will acknowledge their name before his Father and his angels (Rev 3:1-6).

Church 6: The Church of Philadelphia

- **Grade:** Passing

- **Successes:** Jesus knows their good deeds though they only have a little strength. He's pleased they've kept his word and not denied his name.

- **Problems:** None. Jesus is going to show those who have persecuted them that he loves them.

- **To Improve:** None needed though they need to hold on to what they have so no one can take their crown.

- **Reward if Overcomes:** This is the church that will not have to endure the hour of tribulation over the whole earth. Jesus tells them he will make them a pillar in the temple of my God, and he will write on them the name of his God and the name of the city of his God, the new Jerusalem, as well as his new name (Rev 3:7-13).

Church 7: The Church of Laodicea

- **Grade:** Failing

- **Successes:** None. Their deeds are neither hot nor cold and God wants to spit them out of his mouth.

- **Problems:** They are prideful and think they are rich, but they are poor.

- **To Improve:** Jesus counsels them to "buy" from him gold refined in the fire, so they can become rich; and to "buy" white clothes to cover their shameful nakedness; and to "buy" salve for their eyes so they can see. Jesus reminds them he rebukes and disciplines those he loves. He calls them to be earnest and to repent.

- **Reward if Overcomes:** Jesus will give them the right to sit with him on his throne as he overcame and sat down with his Father on his throne (Rev 3:14-22).

There are several striking things about these seven churches. Jesus loves even the churches that are failing (like Laodicea) and gives them hope. Why else would he be walking through the lamp stands trimming the lamps? Another thing that strikes me is how the church of Ephesus is doing everything right, yet is failing because the members are not worshipping from their hearts.

Yikes!

Let's take a look at the major pitfalls we the church should avoid:

Repent From:

- Not worshipping from our heart.
- False teachings.
- False teachers.
- Sin and sexual immorality.
- Eating food offered to idols.
- Apathy or only going through the motions.
- Pride.

Go back and recheck this list. If you see anything like sounds like you on this list, stop and repent now. Next, take a look at what Jesus wants you to embrace.

Embrace:

- Repentance.
- Waking up to your true spiritual condition.
- The testing of our teachers and their teachings.
- Removing or correcting those teachers or teachings that are wrong.
- Service in love.
- Faith.
- Perseverance and not growing weary despite circumstances.
- Good deeds.
- Hating evil.
- Keeping God's commands.
- The testing of our faith.
- Discipline.

Now stop and pray and ask for God to give you his power, favor, and grace in all of these areas.

…This scene in John's vision ends with Jesus saying a remarkable thing to the churches (not the world), "Here I am! I stand at the door and knock. If anyone hears my voice and opens the door, I will come in and eat with him, and he with me. To him who overcomes, I will give the right to sit with me on my throne, just as I overcame and sat down with my Father on his throne. He who has an ear, let him hear what the Spirit says to the churches" (Rev 3:20-22).

He's knocking, can you hear him? So what are you waiting for? Invite him into your life, your home, job, church and circumstances.

A few years ago, I had a reality check concerning Christ's presence. I was home alone during a sudden power surge. The surge somehow kicked started my CD player on to its highest volume. Suddenly in the stillness, the voice of Carmen, the recording artist, rang out a shout, "Jesus Christ is in the house!"

My heart stopped. In that moment, I fully expected Jesus in all his glory to walk up the stairs and look at me. I was ready to hit the floor, face down. But I had another impulse. Though most people would describe me as "a pretty good person, " I was suddenly keenly aware of my sin. Like Adam and Eve when they realized God would see them naked, I fought an impulse to hide.

As the song continued, I realized what happened to my stereo. Though I was aware Carmen's rap came from a CD, I knew "Jesus *was* indeed in my house." That changes everything because his presence changes me.

How would you react if Jesus in his majesty knocked on the door of your house, your life, your ministry, your family, and your church? (Take a moment to reread and reflect on this question.)

Jesus will come in *when* you open the door. Let him wash your robe in his blood, so you can walk in his presence clean and without sin. Go wherever he leads you and overcome.

Jesus as the Lamb Who Was Slain

Before we leave Revelations, let me show you another description of the glorified Jesus. John says,

"Then I saw a Lamb, looking as if it had been slain, standing in the center of the throne, encircled by the four living creatures and the elders. He had seven horns and seven eyes, which are the seven spirits of God sent out into all the earth. He came and took the scroll from the right hand of him who sat on the throne. And when he had taken it, the four living creatures and the twenty-four elders fell down before the Lamb. Each one had a harp and they were holding golden bowls full of incense, which are the prayers of the saints. And they sang a new song" (Rev 5:6-9).

But what does the description, "Lamb of God," mean?

The sacrifice of a lamb was often used in Jewish worship services for the removal of sin. Jesus became our sacrificial lamb. To make that point, when John the Baptist saw Jesus down at the Jordon River he declared in John 1:29, "Look, the Lamb of God, who takes away the sin of the world!"

Jesus is our sacrificial lamb. But why is he depicted with so many horns and eyes in Revelations? "Wm. G. Moorehead said, 'The Lamb has 'seven horns and seven eyes' (5:6), which denote the almighty power, the supreme intelligence, and the perfect omniscience with which He is endowed.'"[56]

But one of the amazing things is God shares his throne and his worship with the Lamb who was slain. What is the new song the elders of heaven are singing to the Lamb? Listen to their voices as the song turns into living music.

---

[56] Wm. G. Moorehead quote from the *Studies in the Book of Revelation* from *The Wycliffe Bible Commentary, Electronic Database*, (Chicago, IL, Moody Publishers, 1962), pp. 30-32.

You are worthy to take the scroll
and to open its seals,
because you were slain,
and with your blood you purchased men for God
from every tribe and language and people and nation.
You have made them to be a kingdom and priests to serve
our God,
and they will reign on the earth (Rev 5:9-10).

Only Jesus is worthy to open the scroll, open the seals of prophecies, and events past and those to come. But not only will the Lamb open the seals, John goes on to describe several things the lamb does, can, or will do including:

- Be worshipped by the same pageantry as the Ancient of Days.
- Open the Book of Life.
- Write names in the Book of Life.
- Blot out names from the Book of Life.
- Remove lamp stands.
- Sit with his father on the throne.
- Open the seals.
- Carry out wrath and judgment.
- Use his blood to cleanse our robes.
- Shepherd and care for those from the great tribulation.
- Overcome.
- Help us overcome with the power of his blood.
- Take his Bride.
- Enter his temple.

Follow the Cloud

The Lamb will also return to earth the same way he left, in a cloud.

Look, he is coming with the clouds,
and every eye will see him,
even those who pierced him;
and all the peoples of the earth will mourn because of him.
So shall it be! Amen (Rev 1:7).

Daniel also writes of this day in Daniel 7:13-14,

"In my vision at night I looked, and there before me was one like a son of man, coming with the clouds of heaven. He approached the Ancient of Days and was led into his presence. He was given authority, glory and sovereign power; all peoples, nations and men of every language worshiped him. His dominion is an everlasting dominion that will not pass away, and his kingdom is one that will never be destroyed."

Come Lord Jesus, come.

Love Notes:

In this chapter we talked about:

- John's vision of the glorified Jesus.
- The message Jesus had for his churches.
- A look to see which church we most represent.
- The portrayal of Jesus as the Lamb of God.
- Notice that Jesus will come again and that his kingdom will never pass away.

Worship Experience:

Experience One:

Meditate on how Jesus refers to himself in his message to the churches.

- Him who holds the seven stars in his right hand and walks among the seven golden lamp stands. (Rev 2:1-2).

- Him who is the First and the Last, who died and came to life again (Rev 2:8).

- Him who has the sharp, double-edged sword (Rev 2:12).

- The Son of God, whose eyes are like blazing fire and whose feet are like burnished bronze (Rev 2:18-19).

- Him who holds the seven spirits of God and the seven stars (Rev 3:1).

- Him who is holy and true, who holds the key of David. What he opens no one can shut, and what he shuts no one can open (Rev 3:7-8).

Experience Two:

John sees a great multitude and hears them sing praise to the Lamb. See if you can spot the seven ways they honor him in this song, then sing this song to him yourself.

"Worthy is the Lamb, who was slain,
to receive power and wealth and wisdom and strength
and honor and glory and praise" (Rev 5:12)!

Chapter 12

Divine Work

"Genuine worship always leads to an outward look — a personal response or action — a desire to be obedient to whatever God calls you to do." – Chip Ingram[57]

Congratulations, you and I have just watched the greatest (and longest-running) mini-series ever created. Here we are at our final episode. (Hey, we have to stop sometime; we were running out of popcorn.)

We've taken an amazing journey together — starting from before time itself. We've witnessed the terrible kidnapping in the Garden of Eden leading to man's separation from God. Finally, we witnessed Jesus' sacrificial death and resurrection that is the key to our reconciliation with God.

This, our story with God, is the greatest romance ever told. The romance of God's love for mankind. How glad I am this story has a happy ending, for you, for me, and for our Lord.

I have a final few clips to share that sheds light on balance.

The Meaning of Balance

It was a lovely Sunday afternoon in April, the perfect day for a two-hour flight between Temple and Beaumont, Texas. I was seated in the small Cessna 210, with a seatbelt that served more as a decoration than a restraint. With my husband at the controls, we sailed upward into the afternoon

---

[57] *Chip Ingram, Worship – the Key To Drawing Near to God* article from Oneplace.com, © Copyright 2006, Oneplace.com. All rights reserved.

sunshine. We'd been in the air for over an hour with the engine purring. I leaned back as I enjoyed a book by Matt Redman, *The Unquenchable Worshipper.*

The ground below glowed emerald green with dark blue river ribbons curling and twisting through farms, forests, and small Texas towns. The sky above was pure blue as we sailed in and out of white, cotton candy-puffs. I turned the page as Matt made an interesting point. "I am convinced that it's possible to work really hard at the tasks God called us to do and still maintain a vibrant, intimate relationship with him. Jesus did...."[58]

I nodded to myself. *True. Jesus did.*

Matt continued, "The key is balancing the times of hard work with times of uninterrupted devotion..."

Balance, I mused, leaning one shoulder on the cockpit door. *That's it.*

POP! The door unlatched and pushed open. A gush of cool air jarred me as I found myself leaning out the open doorway. I could see a small town about eight thousand feet below, located between my elbow and my body.

BALANCE!

I caught myself, leaned inside the aircraft, then grabbed the door handle. I tried to push it out so I could slam the door shut.

Paul said, "Don't even bother. You won't be able to shut the door till we land."

Still, I had to try. When I tried to push again, I froze. I imagined what would happen if I shoved the door open and the wind ripped it off the plane with me still holding onto it.

---

[58] Matt Redman, *The Unquenchable Worshipper, Coming Back to the Heart of Worship,* P. 101.

I stopped shoving and now tugged. I used all my strength to keep the door closed.

"You don't need to do that either. The wind will keep the door closed for you."

I wasn't so sure, so with my right hand I held onto the underside of the seat. I crossed my left arm over my right and gripped the handle, creating a tight brace as I held the door. After a while my arms began to ache from the tension of my embrace with the seat and the door.

"Relax," Paul said. "There's no need to struggle. You couldn't push that door open if you tried."

Suddenly an alarm began to sound in the plane. Paul reached behind his seat for our facemasks. He pulled one out and then fastened the mask's tube to the oxygen valve. He handed it to me.

"What's going on?" I asked.

"That's the carbon monoxide detector. The open door is serving as a suction and the cabin is filling up with carbon monoxide from the outside engine."

Now we really were in danger.

I had to let go of the door so I could put on my protective mask. The door held shut without my help. Soon, I too was safe, breathing pure oxygen. Happily, we landed at the Beaumont airport a few minutes later, without further incident.

Later that night, back at my mom and dad's house, I finished reading the passage on balancing work and worship. It continued, "The key is balancing the times of hard work with times of uninterrupted devotion – moments to be still and know that he is God; times when everything else fades into the background as we sit listening devotedly at the feet of our master."[59]

In light of my earlier adventure, I saw the passage in a fresh light.

As I strove to hold the plane door shut, I needed to let go and let the flow of the wind do it for me. We need to worship God, let go of the results of our work and allow the fresh wind of his spirit to breathe our work to life.

Though I realize I'm called to do the good deeds God prepared in advance for me, I don't have to hold everything together. I need to worship God and allow the fresh wind of the spirit to do the work for and through me.

I cannot control the wind. Neither can I control God. But what I can do is control my response to him. I can take more time to enjoy and recognize his presence so I can more clearly see he is at work in my life, my family, and in the ministry he has privileged me to tend. I can sit at his feet and spend time refreshing my spirit. I can drink deeply of him in praise and quiet reflection of his love and power. I can be still and recognize that he is God.

There are times I need to fight the good fight. Then there are other times I must simply rest in him, acknowledging the battle is his, I am his, and the situation is his. I simply need to stop striving and enjoy him as he displays his majesty. If I'm still fighting the good fight when he has called me to "be still," I will be tempted by pride to believe in my own strength, instead of believing in his strength.

Just as I falsely believed the cockpit door was held shut by my own effort, I will think his battles are won by my own strength. There is a balance between worship, rest, and work. A balance that is a necessity.

---

[59] Ibid.

The Importance of Rest

Do you remember when the Israelites took the Ark of
the Covenant into battle only to have it captured by the
Philistines? The Philistines didn't keep the Ark long because
their idol, Dagon, broke its neck before the Ark and the
people developed tumors and were overrun by rats until
they sent the Ark back to the Israelites. But the Israelites
continued to have trouble respecting the Ark — either
publicly viewing it or transporting it improperly.

For example, once while David was moving the Ark, he
did almost everything right as he led the people in intense
worship while heading the parade towards the gates of
Jerusalem. David forgot only one little thing. The Ark was
designed with a series of rings on either side. The priests
were the only ones allowed to carry the Ark. They slid two
gold-inlayed poles through each set of rings, as per God's
instructions. However instead of the priests, David had a
couple of brothers build a cart for it. After all, the Philistines
sent the Ark home on an unmanned cart pulled by oxen.
David reasoned if a cart would work for the Philistines, a
cart would also work for him. Trouble was that David knew
better.

Things didn't go well with David and the ox-drawn Ark.
At a rough spot in the road, the Ark tipped. Uzzah reached
out to steady it. Upon touching it, Uzzah fell down dead. His
and David's disrespect cost his life. A shocked David placed
the Ark in a nearby home until he could decide what to do.

The next time David tried to move the Ark, he did it the
right way. As the priests carried the Ark on its designated
golden poles, they took six steps, then stopped to worship
and to sacrifice a bull and a fatted calf.

An interesting picture, six steps then worship. It's a
picture of what we're supposed to do. We are supposed to

stop after six days to rest and to worship God on the seventh. It's not a suggestion. It's one of the Ten Commandments.

Do you know what's so amazing about that? God wants to spend time with us. He wants to walk with us and we in turn should want to worship him. We want to worship God because of who he is. We also want to rest in God in our work, our family, and our ministry, so he can be glorified. So we can point to his strength, instead of our own. This is the only way we'll be able to give credit where credit is due.

Work and Worship

Yes, rest is important, but so is our work. According to tradition of the Ten Commandments, we rest one day out of seven, but work the other six days.

Many years ago I took a radio interviewing class from Joel Roberts, a popular secular L.A. talk show host turned media trainer. One day as he was lecturing, he told the class a secret that changed my life. He said, "Did you know that the words *work* and *worship* are the same Hebrew word? He wrote the Hebrew word *Abad* on the chalkboard.

I went home and looked it up in my Greek Hebrew dictionary. Sure enough, I found this definition:

abad (aw-bad'); a primitive root; to work (in any sense); by implication, to serve, till, (causatively) enslave, etc.:

KJV ... (cause to, make to) serve ... (be, become) servant ... work, be wrought, worshipper.[60]

---

[60] Biblesoft's *New Exhaustive Strong's Numbers and Concordance with Expanded Greek-Hebrew Dictionary.*

This means we can exchange the word worship for the words service or work. For example, the NIV of Exodus 9:1 reads:

> *Then the LORD said to Moses, "Go to Pharaoh and say to him, 'This is what the LORD, the God of the Hebrews, says: "Let my people go, so that they may worship me."*

This same Scripture translated in the NKJ version as:

> *Then the LORD said to Moses, "Go in to Pharaoh and tell him, 'Thus says the LORD God of the Hebrews: "Let My people go, that they may serve Me."*

Both translations are correct.

Perhaps this is one of the reasons why Martha got in trouble with Jesus. She didn't view kitchen duty as worship.

Mary and Martha were sisters of Lazarus, a leader in the town of Bethany. Lazarus saw something compelling in this young rabbi and invited him home to dinner. The sisters were excited to entertain the one rumored to be Messiah and worked to prepare a wonderful meal for their soon-to-arrive guest. When the knock came, Mary peeked out of the kitchen. "Jesus is here!" she called over her shoulder and slipped out of the kitchen.

When Martha went to the kitchen door to check, sure enough, Mary sat at the feet of Jesus, listening to his teachings and identifying herself as a follower of Christ. Martha was furious. Left to do all the work, she stuck her head out the kitchen door to complain and—here, I'll roll the tape…

> …"*Lord, don't you care that my sister has left me to do the work by myself? Tell her to help me!*"

"Martha, Martha, you are worried and upset about many things, but only one thing is needed. Mary has chosen what is better, and it will not be taken away from her" (paraphrased Luke 10:38-42).

Here's the truth of the matter. Both women were serving Jesus. Mary was spending time with him, while Martha was working to finish his dinner.

Not only could Martha's work have been counted as worship if she'd had a better attitude, she actually had the best of both worlds; she was about to serve the meal she prepared for the Lord AND sit at his feet. I think we learn from Martha's story that worship is not so much an activity as an attitude.

Send Me

But in truth, it's our love of the Lord that compels us to service. Let's roll this last clip and take a look at Isaiah, the prophet who lived about seven hundred years before Christ. But first, note Isaiah had a very similar experience as John the apostle. He had a vision of the Lord seated on the throne. He saw the seraphs with six wings in the court of the Most High. These angel creations covered their faces with two wings, covered their feet with two wings, and flew with two wings. They called to one another....

..."Holy, holy, holy is the LORD Almighty; the whole earth is full of his glory."

At the sound of their voices the doorposts and thresholds shook and the temple was filled with smoke. Isaiah was suddenly keenly aware of his sin. He cried, "Woe to me! I am ruined! For I am a man of unclean lips, and I live among a people of unclean lips, and my eyes have seen the King, the LORD Almighty."

Then one of the seraphs flew to him with a live coal in his hand, which he had taken with tongs from the altar. The seraphs touched Isaiah's mouth with the coal and said, "See, this has touched your lips; your guilt is taken away and your sin atoned for."

This is symbolic of what Jesus did for us by taking way and atoning for our sin. Now Isaiah was ready for an assignment. The Lord says, "Whom shall I send? And who will go for us?"

Isaiah says, "Here am I. Send me" (Isaiah 6:1-8)!

After Isaiah's vision of God, he was quick to volunteer to carry out God's purposes. Not to earn his redemption, but to serve the God who had humbled and awed him. That's why he gladly accepted the assignment to bring a difficult message to the people.

As our revelation of God and his Son become clear to us, we'll hear a call to serve and we'll respond, "Here am I. Send me!" Yes, God has a purpose for you. Yes, he is asking you to fulfill that purpose. He's calling out to you, "Whom shall I send?"

Do you hear his voice? If you do, pray this prayer:

Dear Lord,

Thank you for revealing yourself to me. Thank you for sending your son Jesus to die on the cross for my sins, to redeem me to yourself. I hear your call, and I say to you, "Yes! I will go. Send me." Lead me, guide me, and help my work to be refined by fire so that it will remain as my work of worship to you.

In Jesus name

Amen

Now that we've studied God's love story with mankind, it's time to write our own personal love story to God. But first, shall we worship?

Love Notes:

In this chapter we talked about:

- Balance in our walk with God.

- Worshiping God with our service.

- Worshiping God by resting and abiding in his presence.

- True worship as an attitude of the heart.

- Responding to God with, "Send me."

Now it's time to write our own personal story with God.

Worship Experience:

God gave you special gifts to carry out the mission he's set aside *for you* from the beginning of time. As you follow God's mission, you may only be able to take the journey one step at a time. However, you will not go empty handed. Not only is the Lord going with you, he's maturing and refining those special gifts.

Take a look at this list of gifts and place up to three stars next to the gift(s) you think God may have given you. (If you don't think you have a particular gift, don't place a star next to it. Place three stars next to a strong gifting.)

If you feel confused as to which gift(s) is yours, you may want to talk to your friends and family to help you discern your gifts. And never fear, God has given everyone gifts. He will not leave you empty handed. The following list is based on 1 Corinthians 12:7-11 and I Corinthians 13.

- Wisdom (clear thinking concerning directives of God and understanding how to direct man.)

- Understanding (understanding how God's word applies.)
- Faith (knowing God is able.)
- Love (loving others.)
- Hope (hoping in God)
- Miraculous powers.
- Gift of healing.
- Prophecy (Understanding truth in current events and the understanding of future events to come.)
- Discernment (If situation or person is from God or not.)
- Speaking in tongues (Speaking to God or others in another tongue.)
- Interpretation of tongues. (Understanding a message spoken in another tongue.)

Now say this prayer, concerning the gifts you've starred.

Dear Lord,

I give these gifts to you. Help me to use them in service of you, to produce good works.

In Jesus Name,

Amen

Experience Two:

Read the following Scripture passage first to understand, then again as a prayer:

As for you, you were dead in your transgressions and sins, in which you used to live when you followed the ways of this world and of the ruler of the kingdom of the air, the spirit who is now at work in those who are disobedient. All of us also lived among them at one time, gratifying the cravings of our sinful nature and following its desires and thoughts. Like the rest, we were by nature objects of wrath. But because of his great love for us, God, who is rich in mercy, made us alive with Christ even when we were dead in transgressions-it is by grace you have been saved. And God raised us up with Christ and seated us with him in the heavenly realms in Christ Jesus, in order that in the coming ages he might show the incomparable riches of his grace, expressed in his kindness to us in Christ Jesus. For it is by grace you have been saved, through faith-and this not from yourselves, it is the gift of God- not by works, so that no one can boast. For we are God's workmanship, created in Christ Jesus to do good works, which God prepared in advance for us to do (Eph 2:1-10).

If you would like to review *The God You Need To Know's* study/discussion questions, please go to:
www.EnjoyGodStory.com

Please pray that this little book can reach a world of people who need to know a God who loves them. Also, prayerfully consider giving *The God You Need to Know* to friends and family so they can discover a loving relationship with their Creator. Together, with your prayers and help, we can make a difference!

For more information on ordering books, go to
www.GotToPray.com.

About the Author

Linda Evans Shepherd is the author of over thirty books including *When You Don't Know What to Pray, Winning Your Daily Spiritual Battles and Praying the Promises* (2018), as well as the bestselling novel series, *The Potluck Club* and *The Potluck Catering Club*, written with Eva Marie Everson. To see a current list of Linda's books, go to this website: www.GotToPray.com

An internationally recognized speaker, Linda has spoken in almost every state in the country and around the world. You can learn more about her speaking ministry at: www.LindaEvansShepherd.com.

Linda is the president of Right to the Heart Ministries. She is the CEO of AWSA (Advanced Writers and Speakers Association,) a ministry to Christian authors and speakers. She also publishes the website GodTest.com, the magazine, Leading Hearts. To get a free subscription, our gift to you, go to: LeadingHearts.com.

Linda has been married to Paul for over thirty years and is the mother of their two children.

To find more information and discover videos and other helps that relate to this book, go to this website www.EnjoyGodStory.com.